Zendoodle
The Mastery Series

33 Zendoodle Patterns to Inspire Your Inner Artist— Even if You Think You're Not One
Volume 1

Olivia Summers

Published in The USA by:

Success Life Publishing

125 Thomas Burke Dr.

Hillsborough, NC 27278

Copyright © 2015 by Olivia Summers

ISBN-10: 1517709385

DISCLAIMER: This book is for educational and informational purposes only. Results vary with every individual, and your results may or may not be different from those depicted. No promises, guarantees or warranties, whether stated or implied, have been made that you will produce any specific result from this book. Your efforts are individual and unique, and may vary from those shown. Your success depends on your efforts, background and motivation.

Table of Contents

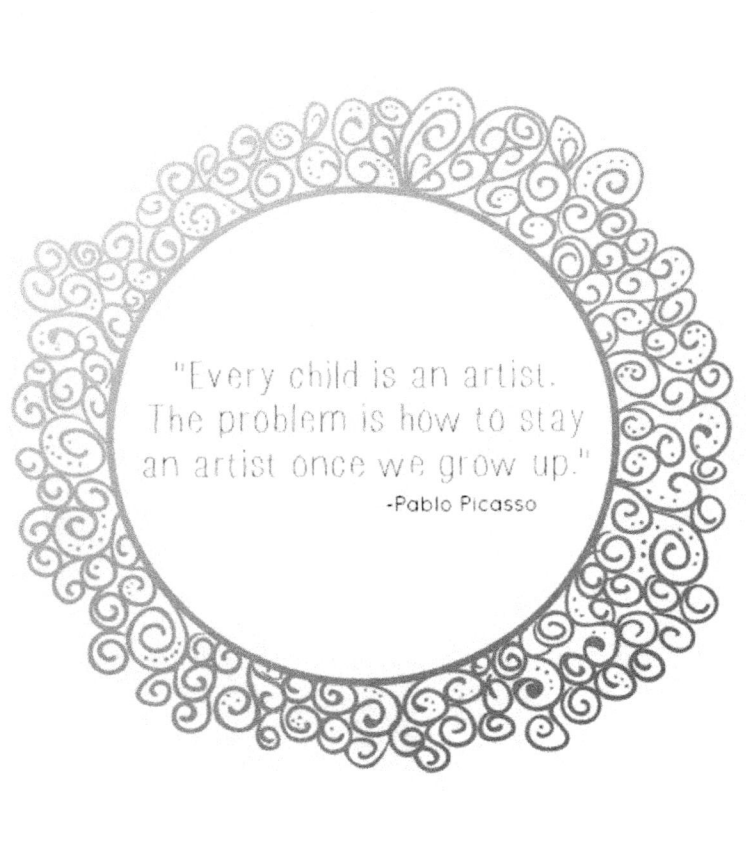

"Every child is an artist.
The problem is how to stay
an artist once we grow up."
-Pablo Picasso

Introduction

Welcome to your journey with the Zendoodle Method. Whether you're brand-new to the practices of Zendoodle, or you're a "doodle" pro, this book is sure to have a little something for everyone.

So what is Zendoodle? Everyone knows what doodling is and we've all been doing it in the margins of our notebooks or, in the case of the ancient Egyptians--on cave walls--since the beginning of time. However, up until a few years ago there was no need to give it a name--it was just something that people did with little thought to who "created" it. But as these drawing practices grew more popular, the term 'Zendoodle' was born. More specifically, Zendoodle is a way of drawing that is focused on creating mindfulness and a meditative state of mind.

When I first heard of it, it wasn't quite as mainstream as it is now, but in the last few years this form of drawing has really picked up steam and gathered quite a following.

To be honest, at first I was skeptical and more than a little intimidated. After all, I am not a "natural" artist. I've never been what I would consider skilled at drawing or painting. I can get by in a game of Pictionary, but that's about the extent of it.

So when I took a class for the first time I was nervous that I would completely blow it. I mean, I didn't want to *totally* suck—but I was afraid that that was what would happen.

As the teacher began teaching the "doodles," as she called them, I was hopeful because—dare I say—this was doable. She deconstructed each pattern step by step and...it was kind of easy. Not easy in a boring way, but easy in a relieving and calming way. I wasn't overwhelmed like I thought I would be.

I have to be honest: the night before I took that first class with her, I was so nervous that I Googled the term 'Zendoodle art.' Well, just like they say to never Google your medical ailments, there should also be a warning label on 'Zendoodle art.'

Although the images that I saw were amazingly beautiful, I thoroughly felt overwhelmed and intimidated. *This* is what I would be doing tomorrow?! The patterns and drawings were so complex and intricate that I thought for sure there would be no way I could ever accomplish something like that. Drawings like the ones I was seeing surely had to take months to complete.

I almost backed out of going to that first class, but I'm glad I didn't. As soon as I sat down and started "doodling" everything seemed to fall into place in my head. All the worry and anxiety I had been having—all the stress—it just faded away. All that mattered in the minutes and hour that followed was each step and perfecting it.

At the end of Jen's class I was *so* proud of myself. I looked at my drawings and couldn't believe that these drawings came from *my* pen. Not to mention, that something in black and white could be so beautiful (I'm addicted to color).

From then on, I was hooked on Zendoodle and I still am! I never thought that someone like me—who "doesn't draw"— turned into someone who does Zendoodle and creates beautiful works of art...step by step.

I'm sharing my story with you in hopes that it will inspire you to give Zendoodle a try—even if you believe you aren't an artist.

I urge you to give the step-by-step patterns in this book a try and see for yourself how easy it really can be!

Zendoodle 101

Who Created It?

No one really knows "where" it came from. After all, like I said, it's simply just a form of doodling that became popular--stuff we've all been doing for years, but with more focus. I have a suspicion that the term Zendoodle stemmed from the fact that there was a lot of confusion about the Zentangle brand (which is copyrighted by Rick Roberts & Maria Thomas) and its uses-- as such Zendoodle was born!

What Exactly *is* the Zendoodle Method?

The Zendoodle Method is a relaxing and easy-to-learn way of creating beautiful artwork from simple step-by-step patterns.

The best part is: there are no rules! Draw what you feel.

Characteristics of Zendoodle Art

- Intuitive

- Ritualistic

- Timeless

- Surprising and unexpected results

- Fun and relaxing

- Easy to practice anywhere

- Non-technical

Benefits of Practicing the Zendoodle Method

- Promotes relaxation

- Improves hand-eye coordination

- Helps change mood and modify behaviors

- Alleviates Insomnia (especially when drawing before bed)

- Promotes mindfulness

- Anger management

- Helps curb food cravings and addictive eating patterns

- Beautiful works of art to display or give to friends and family

- Develops creativity

- Provides a source of inspiration

- Helps combat panic attacks

- Improved self-esteem

- Therapy

- Development and rehab for fine motor skills

- Increased attention span and concentration

- Home schooling

- Problem solving

- Way to warm up for other types of art

Doodle Terminology

Be a know-it-all and use this as a reference guide to all those weird and crazy words that pertain to all things Zendoodle! You can refer back to this section throughout the book if you see a word that you don't recognize.

Aura—One of six enhancement ideas you can use in your drawings. It involves tracing a line around the outside or inside of a given doodle pattern. This is called an aura.

Border—This is where your Zendoodle starts! Lightly pencil a dot in each corner of your tile, then very lightly connect them at the edges to "frame" your tile.

Deconstruct—The process of reducing a pattern to its simplest form (step by step) so that a Zendoodle practitioner can recreate or reconstitute the pattern in a structured sequence.

Dewdrop—One of six enhancement ideas you can use in your drawings. The process involves drawing a circle over your artwork in order to magnify the pattern to give it the illusion of a dewdrop on the page.

Enhancement—Ways to enhance your artwork. Examples

include Aura, Sparkle, Rounding and Dewdrop.

Ensemble—Two+ tiles that can be placed together to look like they're all one sheet or drawing (they share common strings).

Mosaic—When two+ Zendoodle tiles are placed together, all edges touching, resulting in a mosaic.

Perfs—One of six enhancement ideas you can use in your drawings. It's the act of drawing circular borders around your doodles.

Rounding—One of six enhancement ideas you can use in your drawings. It's a variation of shading.

Shading—One of six enhancement ideas you can use in your drawings. It involves lightly penciling shadows and highlights on your doodles to add depth and dimension.

Sparkle—One of six enhancement ideas you can use in your drawings. Adding "sparkle" gives the illusion of your doodle shining in the sun.

String—This is Step 2 of drawing a doodle. It's simply a random free-form line drawn in pencil, within the border you created in Step 1. This is where you draw your doodles.

Doodle—a verb that refers to creating Zendoodle art through the use of doodle patterns. It is meant to be abstract and non-representational. The pattern is created with (at most) 2 or 3 elemental strokes.

Doodle Enhancer—One of several different embellishment techniques used to enhance doodles. Enhancements include aura, shading, dewdrop, perfs, rounding and sparkle.

Tile—A 3 ½" x 3 ½" square "tile" of high quality cardstock that is the basic format for a Zendoodle. They're called tiles because, one finished, they can be formed into a mosaic.

Zendala—This term is a mash-up of the terms Zendoodle and Mandala. A Mandala is (in Hindu and Buddhist cultures) a geometric figure that represents the universe. Zendalas combine the techniques used in Zendoodle artwork and place them inside circular Mandalas.

Zendoodle-Inspired Art (ZIA)—Pretty much any form of Zendoodle that is practiced on any format other than the tiles designed for the purpose of Zendoodle. This could be fabric, wood, metal, a sketchbook, etc.

Common Misconceptions About Zendoodle

The Zendoodle Method is a fun and relaxing way to create beautiful works of art, that just so happen to be easy to learn. Because the finished result often looks complicated, many people are afraid (like I was) to even attempt it.

The good news is that Zendoodle is simply a process of drawing structured patterns, step by step—one stroke at a time. And although it's easy to do, it's far different than simply doodling.

Here are a few of the common myths and misconceptions about the Zendoodle practice.

#1. Zendoodle is only for artists.

In Zendoodle, one of the most beautiful and rewarding parts is that there are **NO** mistakes! Yes, you read that right. And for someone like me this was a big "hallelujah!" moment. I mess up. A lot.

But in Zendoodle it doesn't matter. Either you can find a way to blend it into whatever direction you're going with your doodle, or you can embrace the imperfectness.

After all, doodles are like snowflakes: no two are ever the same! Make it uniquely you. One of the basic premises of Zendoodle drawings is that it's a surprise—even to the person drawing it. When you come out on the other side and stare down at your finished doodle, it's meant to be awe-inspiring. You'll be thinking to yourself, "How did those little strokes and steps develop into *that?*" And that's something to be proud of!

#2. Zendoodle is just a collection of patterns.

When I first started doodling, I actually found myself becoming addicted to collecting patterns and as silly as it might sound, I'm not alone. A lot of doodlers go through the same experience. And although it can be exciting to discover and "collect" new patterns and ideas...the point of Zendoodle is to nurture and foster your *own* personal creativity—not just copy straight from another person's ideas. To be a true piece of Zendoodle artwork, you need to add and develop your own creative flair to each piece and that requires stepping away from the rule book!

I believe it was Cris Letourneau who likened doodle patterns to a box of paints. She said, "If you only use the colors straight from the box, you'll always be limited in your choices. However, when you learn to mix the paints to create your own unique colors, the only limit is your imagination."

As a beginner, it's natural to want to practice and "perfect" the more common doodles, but I urge you to be lenient and kind to yourself. Give your pen the ability to create from your soul and you can never go wrong!

#3 Zendoodle is just "mindless doodling."

First of all, Zendoodle is the complete opposite of mindless doodling—even if it doesn't look like it on the surface.

One of the biggest separating factors between Zendoodle and merely doodling is that Zendoodle is a completely focused and *mindful* form of drawing...whereas doodling is *mindless*.

Now, I'm not saying that there's anything wrong with mindless doodling—it's okay to want to tune out every once in awhile. I'm simply just clearing up any misunderstanding that Zendoodle and simply doodling are one in the same. It's just simply not true.

When you follow the Zendoodle method, every stroke of your pen is deliberate and intentional—which is why it's so incredibly relaxing. For however long you're doodling you can simply draw away all your stresses and worries and focus solely on creating. And we all know that the more we try to forget about our problems or stresses...the more we tend to think about them. The art of doodling will give your brain a much-needed rest.

#4 Doodling is hard and I don't have the proper materials.

With Zendoodle, there is NO excuse not to do it! And I mean that quite literally. Unlike many other forms of artistry, you don't need a lot of time, money, space...or even talent.

So like I said: no excuse. Are there materials and resources it's helpful to have while doodling? Of course. Are they absolutely necessary? Nope.

Really all you need is a pen or sharpie and some sketch paper.

The Method & Materials

The actual process of Zendoodle is simple, but also powerful. It's a ritual of sorts and should be respected from start to finish. As we covered before: it's *not* mindless doodling. Take care during the process to be *mindful* of each stroke and honor your creativity.

The following chart outlines the Zendoodle process from start to finish and should answer any questions you may have about *how* to create a Zendoodle.

The Zendoodle Method

The chart on the next page will quickly explain the Zendoodle Method before we go into more detail.

Step 1: Calm	Before you start doodling, take a minute or two to prepare your mind. If you need to, take a few deep breaths and smile at the opportunity to relax your mind and express yourself.
Step 2: Frame	Lightly pencil in a dot at each of the four corners of your tile or workspace, then connect them to form a border.
Step 3: String	Draw a free-form line in the area inside of your frame, but do it lightly! You can draw one or more lines—just get creative.
Step 4: Doodle	Start out using your pen to fill each section of your string(s) with doodles. This is the fun part!
Step 5: Enhance	After you've finished your doodles, be sure to add enhancements like shading or auras to really make your artwork pop.
Step 6: Finish	Next, add your initials to the front of your artwork and also turn it over and sign your name and date it—you can even write *where* it was created.
Step 7: Appreciate	Finally, take a minute to really look at the big picture and admire the art that you just created. Be proud of your work!

Step 1: Calm

During the first step of the Zendoodle process, it's important to get your mind energized and focused on what's to come.

There should be no worry about past stresses—forget about the fight you just had with your best friend, or the customer who was rude to you at work today...none of that matters in this moment!

Prepare your entire self for the ritual you're about to perform—the cleansing, if you will, of your soul. This all might sound a little extreme to you, but if you truly take time to honor Step 1 in the Zendoodle process, you'll get much more out of each doodle session and feel much more at peace afterward.

It might sound crazy, but I sometimes take about 5 minutes before I doodle, just to do some Breath Awareness meditation. Do you have to do this? Not at all, but I find that it helps to elevate my doodle process and improve the benefits that I get from doodling.

Step 2: Frame

Frames are intended to be a guide, or anchor, to your doodles.

Because there are no rulers or rigid lines to follow in the Zendoodle process, your frame will help guide you throughout the progression of your artwork.

Not to mention, the frame (or border) also aides in being the template for your string that you draw in Step 3.

First, draw four dots (*lightly*) in each edge of your tile or workspace as shown below.

Dots in place.

Next, *lightly* sketch four "sides" connecting the dots to create your frame or border as shown in the picture below.

Finished frame.

Step 3: String

As we just talked about, your string is placed inside your border. The purpose of the string, is to provide a unique template for your Zendoodle artwork.

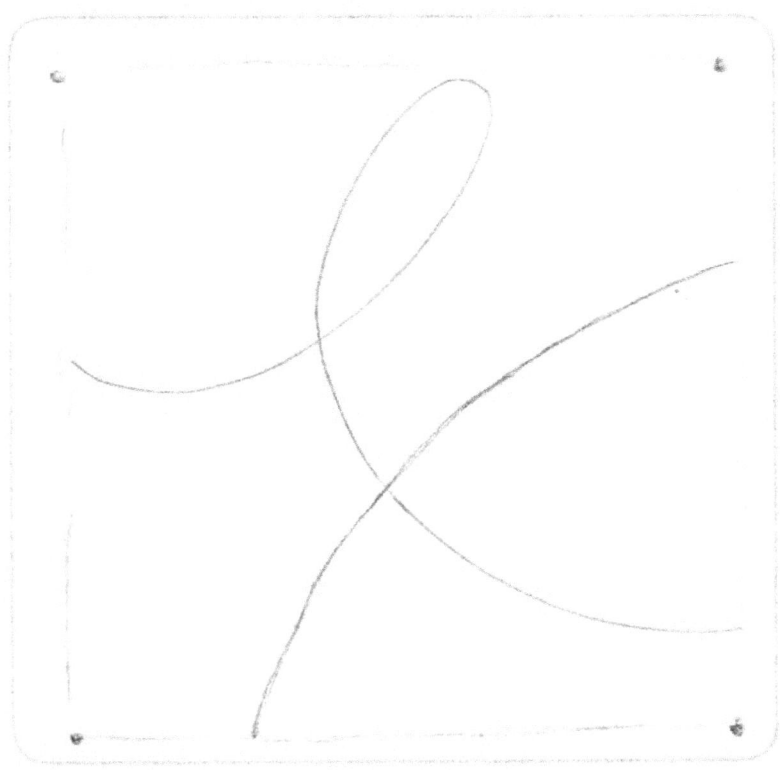

A finished example of a frame with a string, ready to be doodled!

By drawing a string inside your border, you're taking the guesswork and thinking out of where to put each doodle, since your string automatically provides "sections" for each doodle you draw. Pretty cool, huh? It's important to note that once your artwork is completed, the string should blend in with the rest of your piece and you shouldn't really be able to tell where it's at.

A string could be as simple as a geometric shape (like a triangle), or as complicated as a stencil traced over the doodle tile for you to fill in. The purpose of strings are to ensure that your doodle is unique and complex...and never boring!

Ideas for strings include:

- A monogram
- Letters of the alphabet
- Geometric shapes
- French Curves (drawing templates)
- Quilt patterns
- Pre-strung tiles
- Ideas from other Doodlers online

Some String Examples

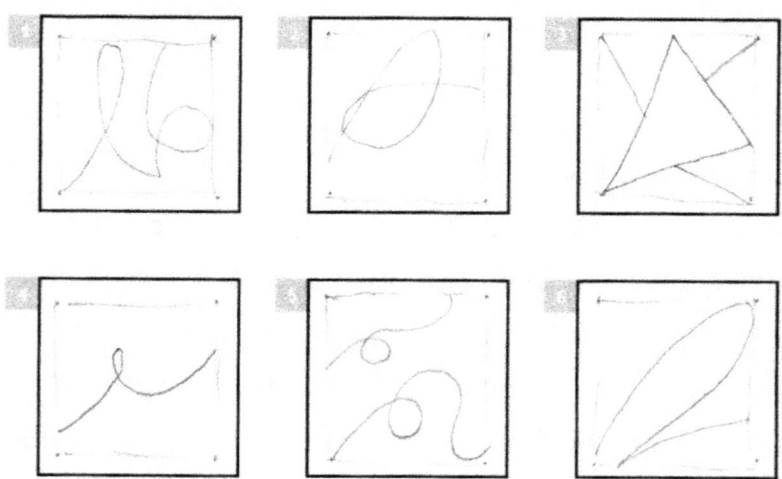

Really, when it comes to strings, the sky is the limit! So get creative and have fun with it, because there really is no wrong way to do it. Well, except for a straight line—don't do that, since it can make for a pretty boring piece of (un)doodled artwork!

Step 4: Doodle

This is the fun part! And what all the previous steps lead up to. Essentially, Step 4 is a creative and free-to-be process.

In this step, you'll use the patterns within this book to create Zendoodle artwork by drawing the patterns of your choosing to fill in the string that you just created. Again, when it comes to the doodle patterns used, the sky is the limit!

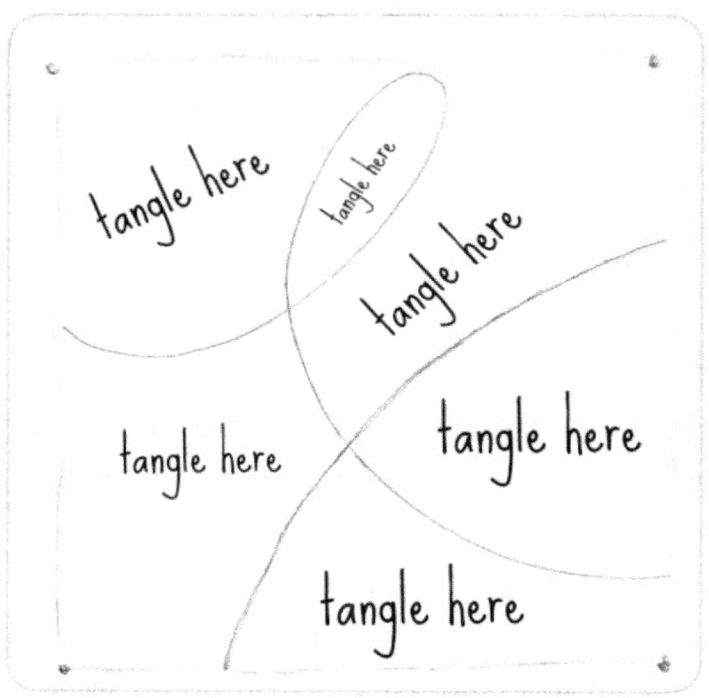

An example showing where to draw each doodle pattern within your string. ('Tangle' is just another word for doodle)

Let your creativity be your guide. Remember: the patterns provided here from the Zendoodle Method are just examples and inspiration. If you're just starting out, you might feel most comfortable to simply "copy" the patterns the way that you see them into your artwork.

However, I hope as time goes on that you will learn to use them as inspiration instead and let your own mind take over and interpret each doodles' meaning for *your* drawings.

Doodle tips:

- **Typically, doodles are done in black and white—**however, you can "enhance" your artwork with art markers, colored pencils, etc. Materials are talked about in the next section.

- **Remember to turn your tile as you work!** Some doodle patterns are much more difficult and confusing than they need to be without turning your tile—so keep that in mind if you're struggling.

- When just starting out, it's best to **choose 3-4 doodle patterns to use** during your drawing session, otherwise it can become quite complicated and overwhelming. When in doubt, keep it simple.

- **Doodles are meant to be abstract and not represent any specific object or form.** Therefore, you should be able to turn it any which way and it "make sense." There is no 'up' on a doodle.

Step 5: Enhance

During Step 5 of the Zendoodle Method, you'll have the opportunity to enhance your doodles that you just created.

Again, in this step, the choices are limitless and can be a bit overwhelming when first starting out on your doodle journey.

I suggest simply starting with black and white doodles until you get comfortable with the process.

Once you feel confident in your basic doodling abilities—play around with enhancements! Spice up your artwork with Perfs, Shading, Auras, Dewdrops, Sparkle or Rounding.

In this step you can even add color—either throughout the whole piece, or simply just pops of color here and there.

Another idea is adding borders around the "frame" of your artwork to create interest and excitement and make your Zendoodle tile stand out.

Although there are many options for enhancements, I feel that 9 times out of 10, less is more. *Could* you use all 6 enhancements, add a border and color your artwork? Yes. *Should* you? Probably not! Oddly, in many scenarios, the more you add to a doodle the less interesting it becomes.

You can find enhancement examples and borders later in this book.

Step 6: Finish

This step is really about authenticating your artwork. Here, you will initial the front of your doodle and then sign and date the back of it.

Many doodlers come up with a creative and fancy way to initial their artwork and "make it their own." If you look at Maria's doodles, you'll know instantly that they're hers, because of her unique initials on the front of the tile.

On the back of your artwork, you'll also want to add your signature and the date it was completed, for reference purposes.

I even like to add *where* my doodle was created so that I can look back and remember exactly when and where I was when I created it. For example: in a meeting, on a flight to NYC, while talking on the phone with my Great Aunt Sue...you get the picture!

Step 7: Appreciate

Often, I think many of us forget this integral step of the Zendoodle process. And that's unfortunate, because I think it's *so* important.

Remember, when you've finished your doodled artwork and you're about to go about the rest of your day, to truly *look* at the finished piece you've just created.

It's quite amazing if you think about it—that you just created this beautiful piece of artwork from nothing. That's part of the beauty of Zendoodle—that art just sort of appears before your very own eyes.

Sure, you *know* that you're creating something in that moment, but you don't realize *what* that something is going to be until it's done. So please, please take a minute or two or five to really appreciate what you've just accomplished and admire your creative process! You deserve it.

That's it! You've just completed the entire process of the Zendoodle Method. Congratulations!

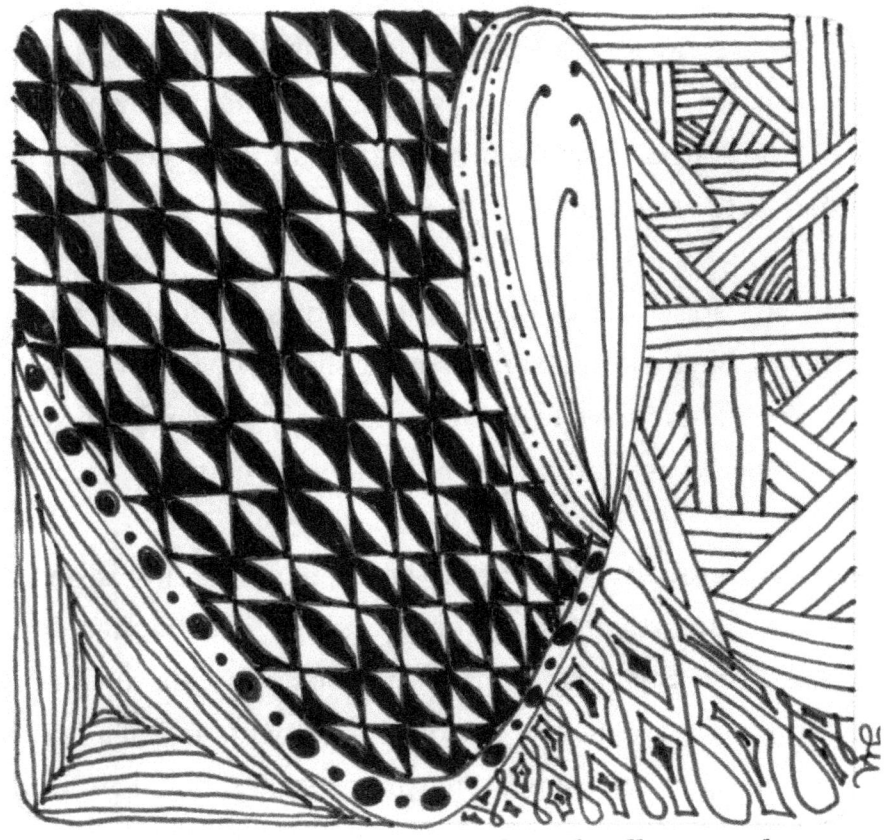

Example of a finished piece of Zendoodle artwork.

The Materials

As I said before...really all you *truly* need to practice Zendoodle is a pen and some paper. However, if you're going to take it seriously and make it a permanent hobby or even give your artwork away as gifts or make some money off of it, then I highly recommend investing from the get-go in quality materials to work with.

There are some things that you can skimp on and cheap out with, but the tools of a serious artist should be an investment. So take the time now, to get your materials gathered and you'll already be set up for a successful Zendoodle journey.

Archival Quality Ink Pens—For Zendoodle, this is one of the most important things you can spend your money on: a great set of archival (or Micron) ink pens. After all, the quality of your artwork depends on your instrument. Yes, it's fine to start out using fine tipped Sharpie pens...but you'll find that these bleed and don't provide as much precision that some of the more detailed patterns require.

Here's a guideline for pen numbers and their thickness:

005 pen = 0.20 mm point

01 pen　 = 0.25 mm point

02 pen　 = 0.30 mm point

03 pen　 = 0.35 mm point

05 pen = 0.45 mm point
08 pen = 0.50 mm point

Gel Pens—Gel ink pens are great for finishing off your artwork and adding the final details or accents. Why? Because the ink is pigment suspended in water-based gel which provides a wonderfully thick, opaque color. This is especially great for already colored, or darker surfaces. Just be sure to let it dry thoroughly as you go since they do smear quite easily. You don't want to ruin your finished artwork with a simple mistake!

Colored Pencils—These are a great tool to use to apply color to your doodled artwork. However, I'm not talking Crayola, here. You'll want to use professional-grade colored pencils. What's the difference? The quality! A good set of colored pencils will have a soft and waxy lead that is great for building layers of color or shading. You can even get a set of watercolor pencils for different effects.

Professional Art Markers—These provide thick, bold, vibrant bands of color and they're wonderful for filling in large areas that need a swatch of color. Believe it or not, you can also use them for shading. I suggest going with Prismacolor brand or something of similar quality.

Pencils—You can use any old pencil you have lying around to draw your strings or create borders in your Zendoodle artwork, but again, I recommend investing a few bucks in some art-specific pencils—especially if you like to shade with them. When picking pencils, it's important to know that they're rated on a hardness/softness scale. 'H' pencils are hard and will make the lightest marks, whereas 'B' pencils are soft and make the darkest marks. The scale is as follows: very soft (9B) to very hard (9H).

Sketchpads & Paper—This is the second most important aspect of your Zendoodle artwork: paper. If you're going to use paper then get a good variety of quality drawing paper—they'll be lots of choices. My suggestion, though is to get a good, sturdy perforated sketchbook to do your doodling in. You can use it as a sort of "doodle journal" and then all your artwork will be handy and in one place and you won't have to worry about losing any drawings like you would with loose-leaf paper.

Zendoodle Tiles—These are specifically made to showcase your doodles and made of thick, heavy-duty cardstock. The appeal here is that they're made from great quality paper that makes your drawings pop. Not to mention, they're typically in the 3 ½" x 3 ½" standard doodle tile size for quick and easy artwork. These are also useful to create "mosaics" with different tiles placed together as one big art piece.

Blending Stumps—These tools simply allow you to soften or blend lines and other areas of your artwork. Although it's a simple gesture, sometimes it can really add dimension to your doodles.

Erasers—Generally speaking, erasers are kind of taboo when it comes to Zendoodle artwork since one of the "rules" is that there aren't any mistakes. However, sometimes in order to clean up your artwork, it does require erasing old sketch lines so it's important to have a good quality eraser to do the trick without smudging the rest of your doodle. My eraser of choice are the moldable and shapeable kind—called kneaded erasers. The beauty of these is that they don't smudge and can be shaped (even into a fine point) to reach delicate places in your art.

Pencil Sharpener—Always a good bet to have one of these around to ensure that your pencils (and colored pencils) are in tip-top shape for your doodles.

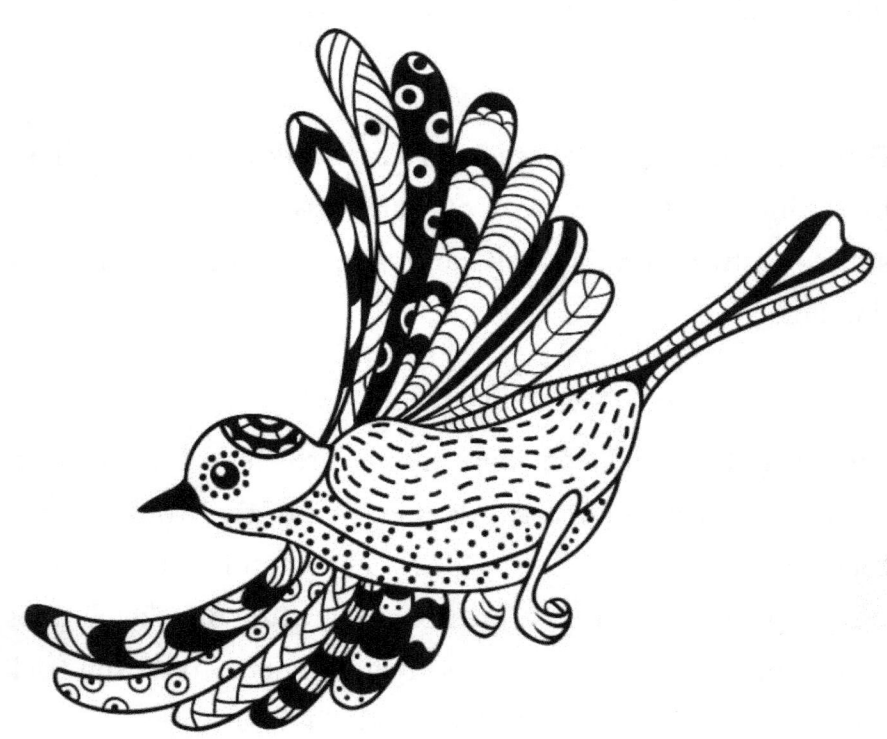

Techniques & Enhancements

After you create your doodles, you'll probably want to add different techniques and enhancements to your artwork to really give them personality and dimension. If you want your doodles to pop, then this chapter will cover all you need to know!

Borders

Here are some example borders you can use in your artwork. With these, the sky is the limit and there are infinite combinations and designs that you can come up with to spice up your doodles.

Use these as a starting point and let your creativity be your guide!

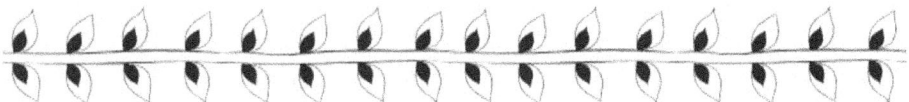

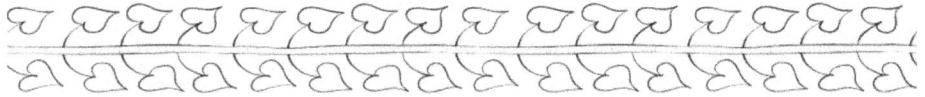

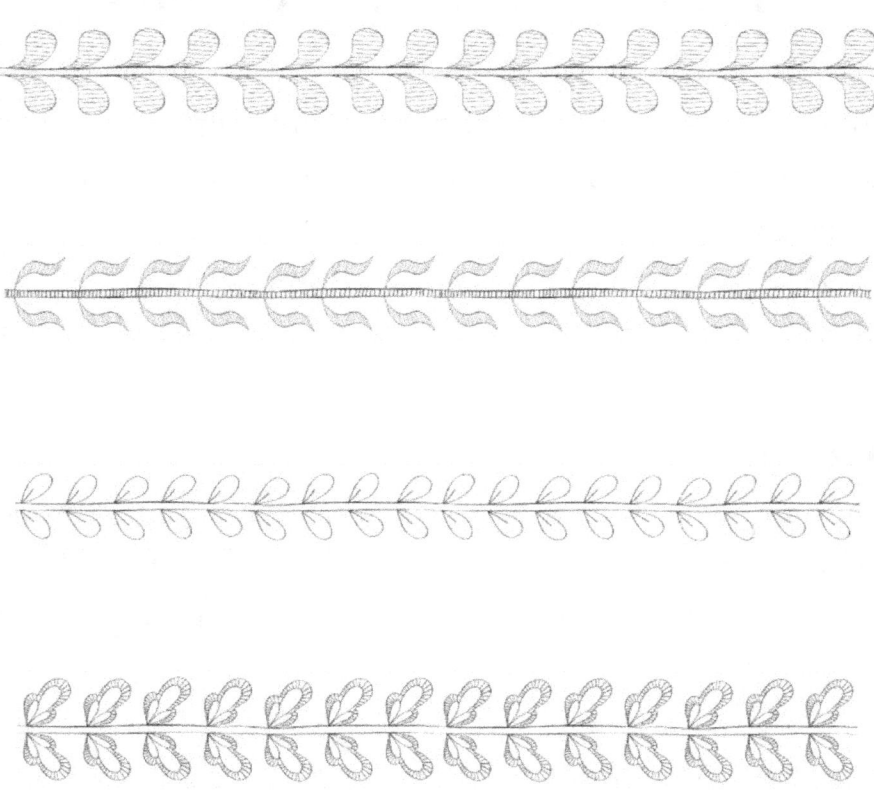

Enhancements

As discussed previously, the following six enhancements can be added to your doodle patterns to create dimension and depth. They also do a good job of making your Zendoodle art stand out from the crowd and give you a creative advantage.

Although you can use as many as you want in a piece of

Zendoodle artwork, often simple is best. I'd stick with only 1-2 enhancements per piece to avoid chaos and clutter.

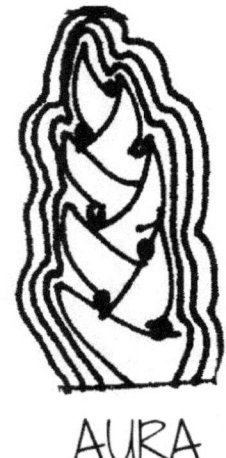

AURA

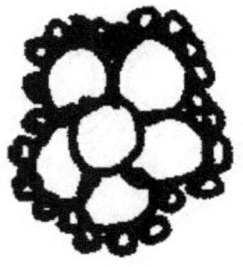

PERFS

ROUNDING

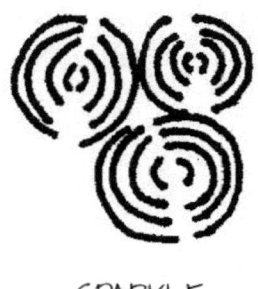

SPARKLE

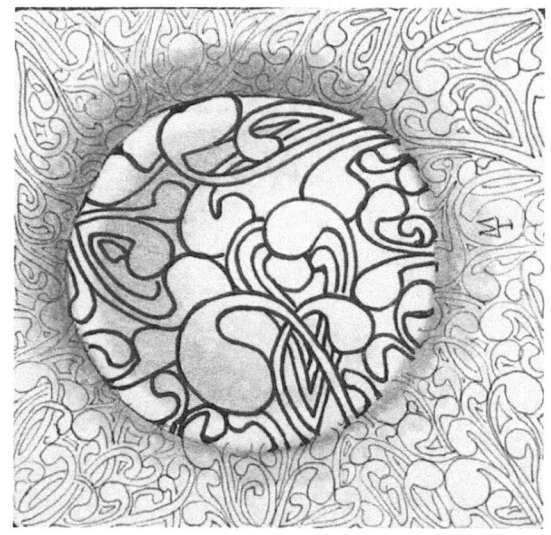

Dewdrop

Source: Maria Thomas

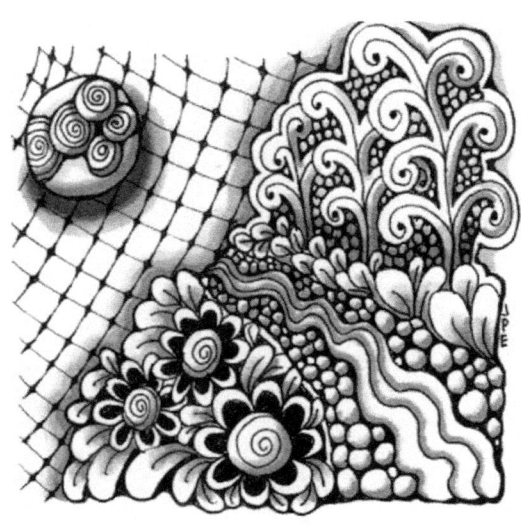

Shading

Source: Google images

Keep all these techniques in mind for when you finish your artwork and think it needs a little something extra. The six enhancements and techniques, along with the border designs will serve you well. Who knows, they might even inspire you to develop your own technique!

"ANYTHING IS POSSIBLE.
ONE STROKE AT A TIME."

quote from zentangle.com

33 Doodle Patterns—Step by Step

I'm sure this is the chapter you've really been waiting for and the whole reason you bought this book. I get it: learning new doodles or simply just starting out can be an exciting time during your journey.

It's important to note that in the Zendoodle Method, each pattern process is illustrated with a wordless picture tutorial. This is done for simplicity. No doodle pattern should be so complicated that it *requires* words to explain it.

With that said, remember to stay mindful and intentional during your doodling experience. Are you ready? Let's get doodled!

A Quick Warm-Up

Before we get started with the pattern how-to's, warm up your hand and pen with these quick strokes to get your creative juices flowing and help you get comfortable with how it feels to perform the different strokes.

No need to stress! This is just for practice. Have fun and loosen up.

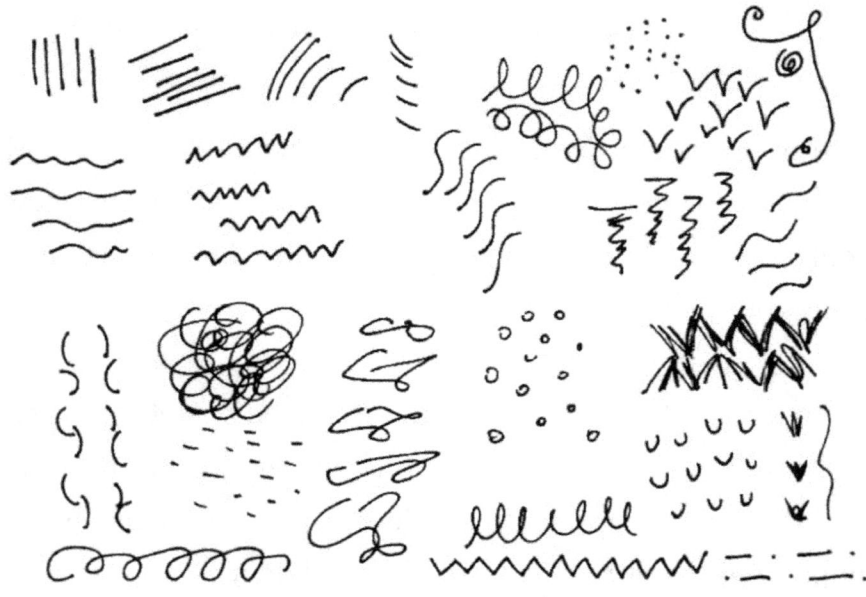

A few things to keep in mind...

- The new, bolder line in each panel is indicative of the next step in the pattern.

- Your finished pattern probably won't look exactly like *my* end result—and that's okay!

- There are NO mistakes.

- Remember to turn your tile as you draw.

- And most importantly...have FUN!

Pattern #1: Paradox

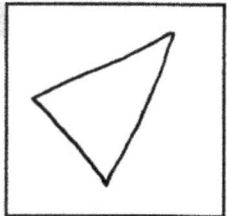 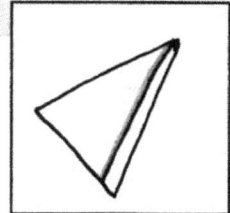 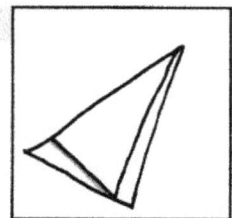

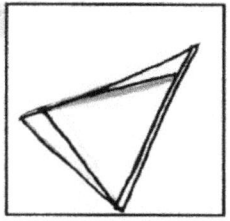 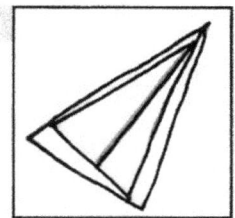 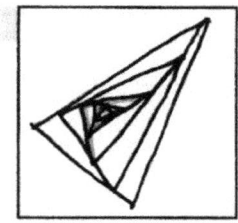

Practice the Steps Below

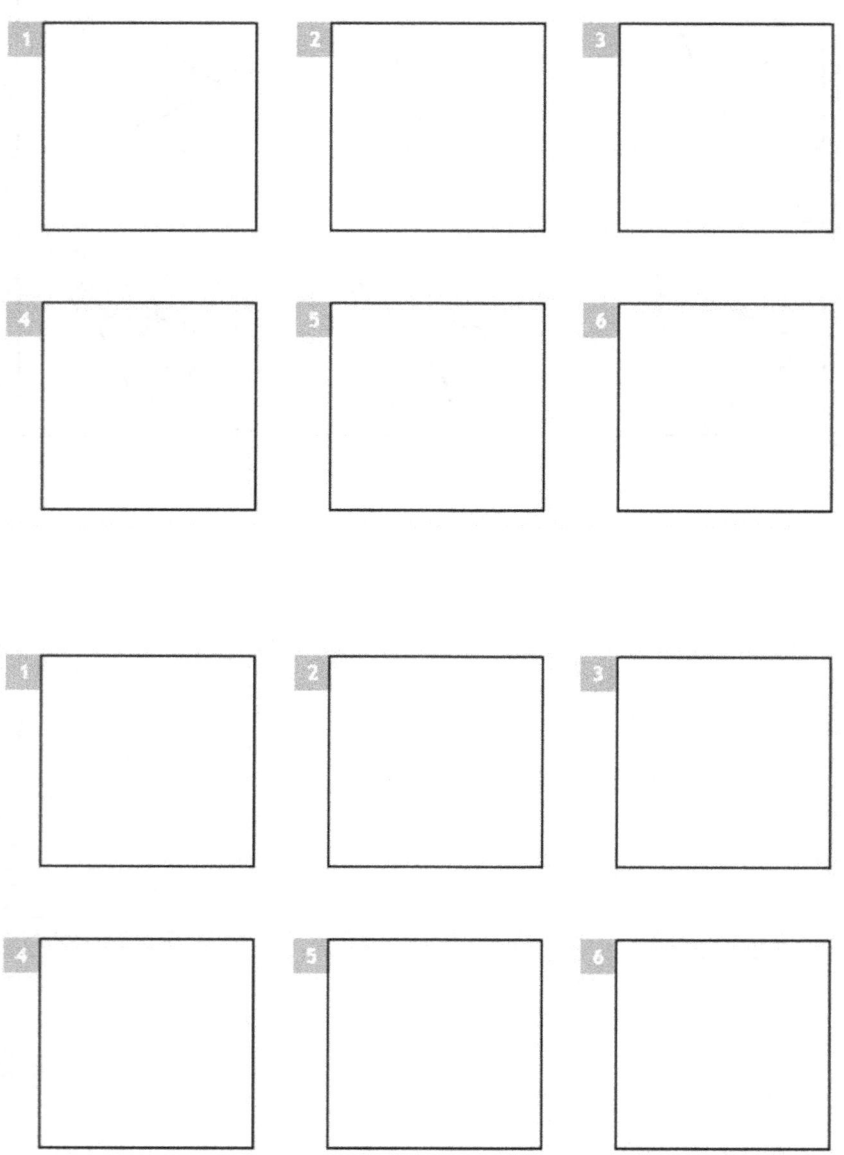

Make Your Own Doodle
Using the Pattern

Pattern #2: Flux

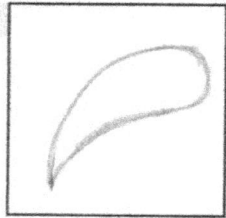 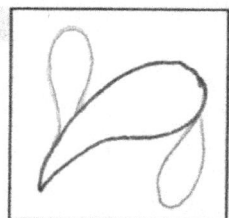 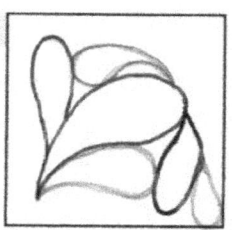

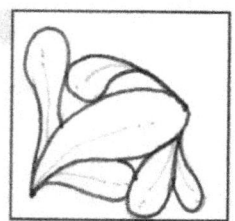 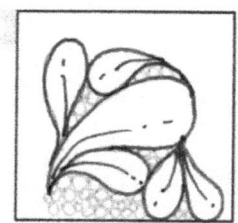 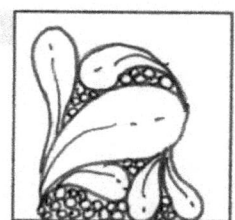

Practice the Steps Below

Make Your Own Doodle
Using the Pattern

Pattern #3: Zinger

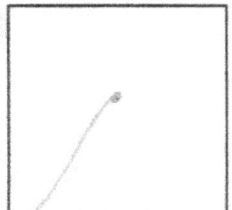 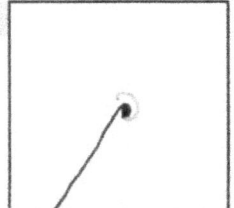 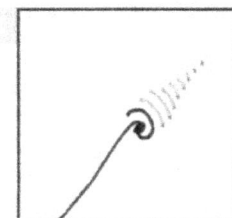

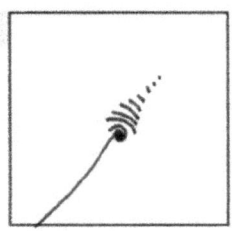

Practice the Steps Below

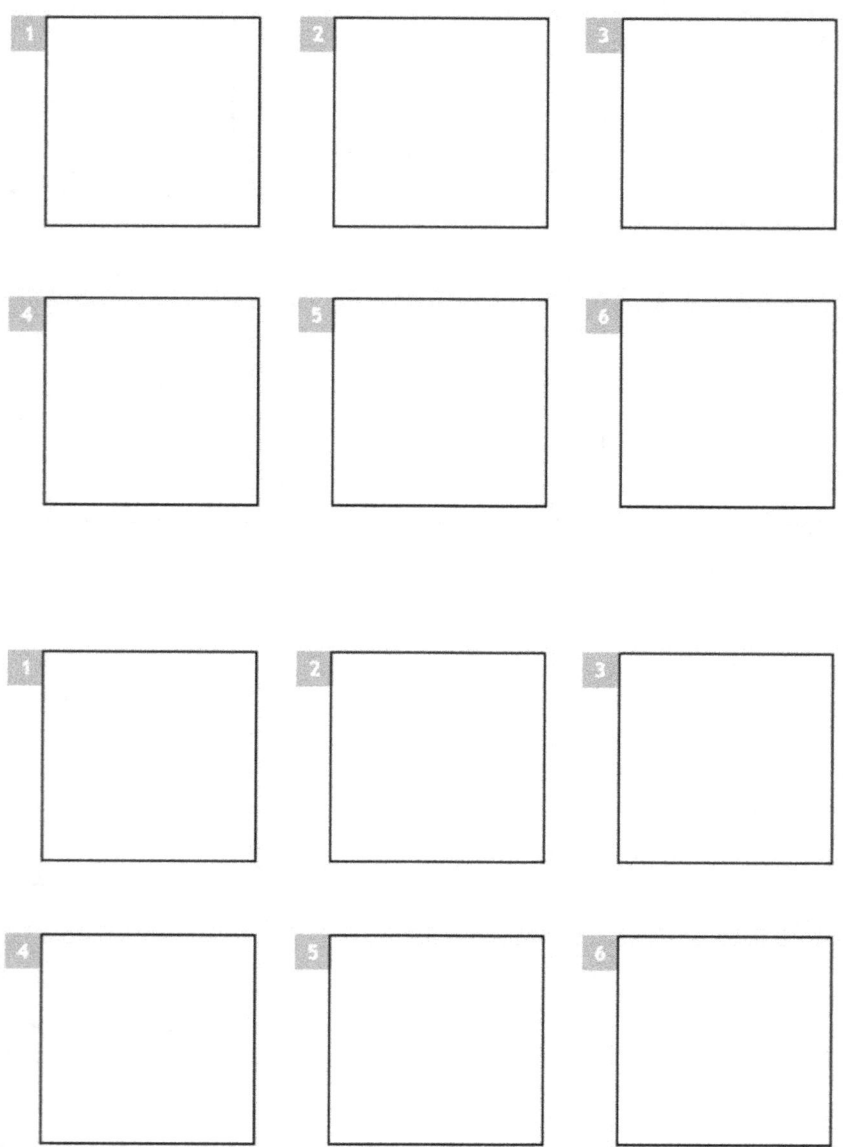

Make Your Own Doodle
Using the Pattern

Pattern #4: Eye-Wa

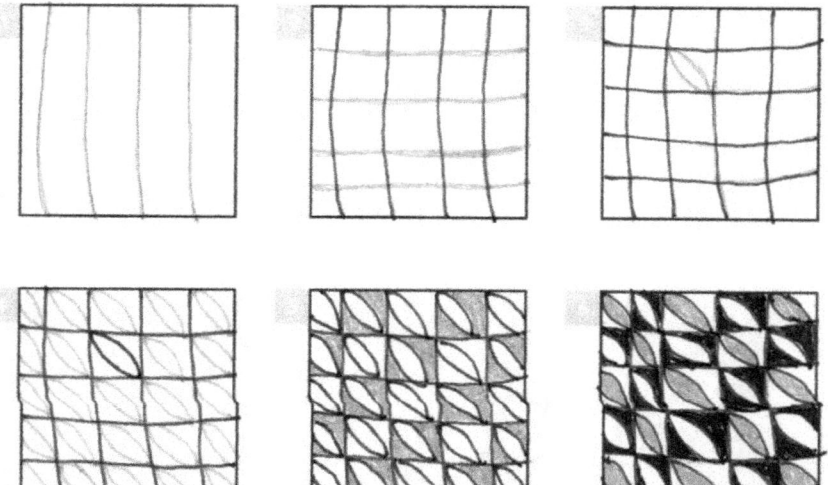

Practice the Steps Below

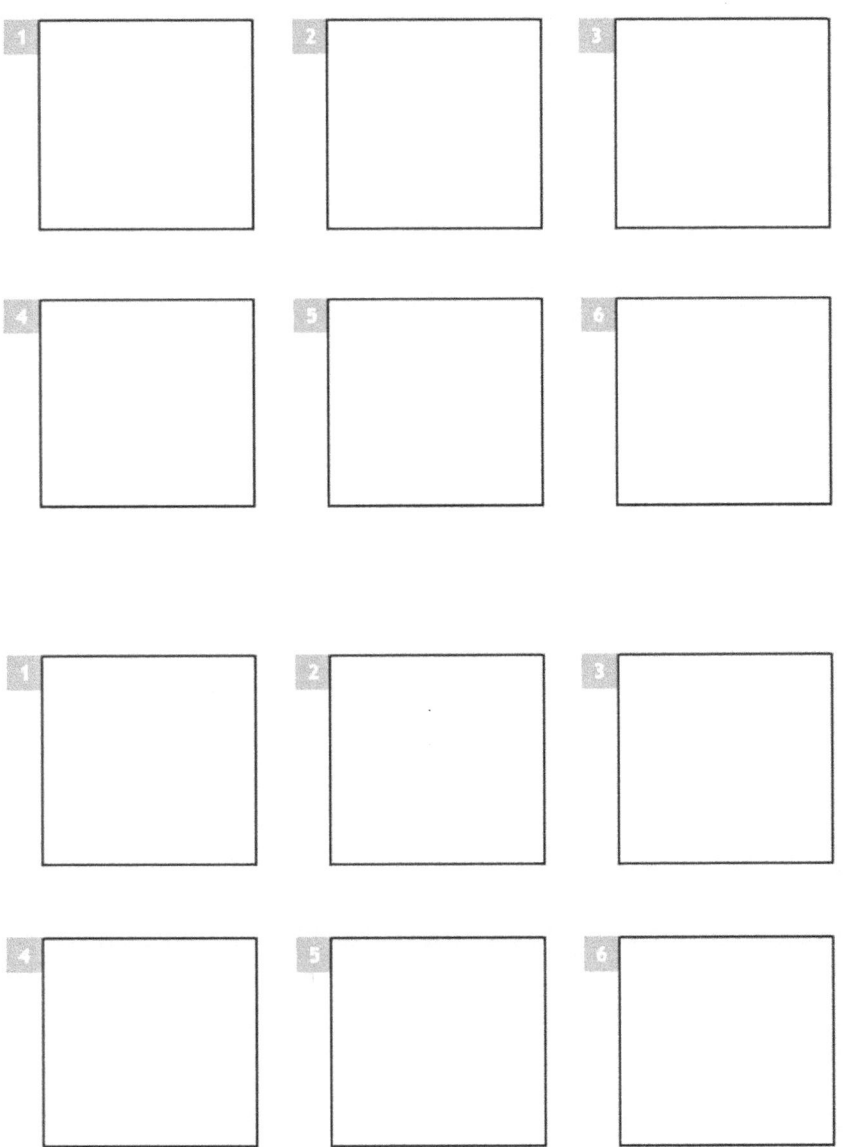

Make Your Own Doodle
Using the Pattern

Pattern #5: Meer

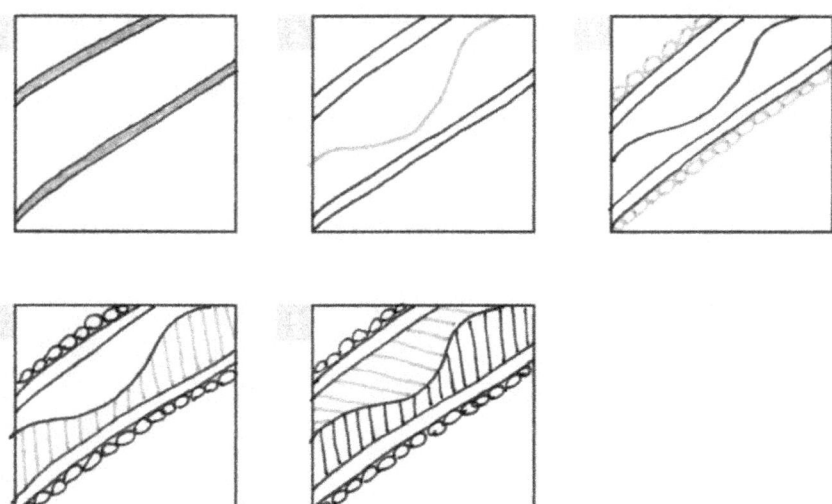

Practice the Steps Below

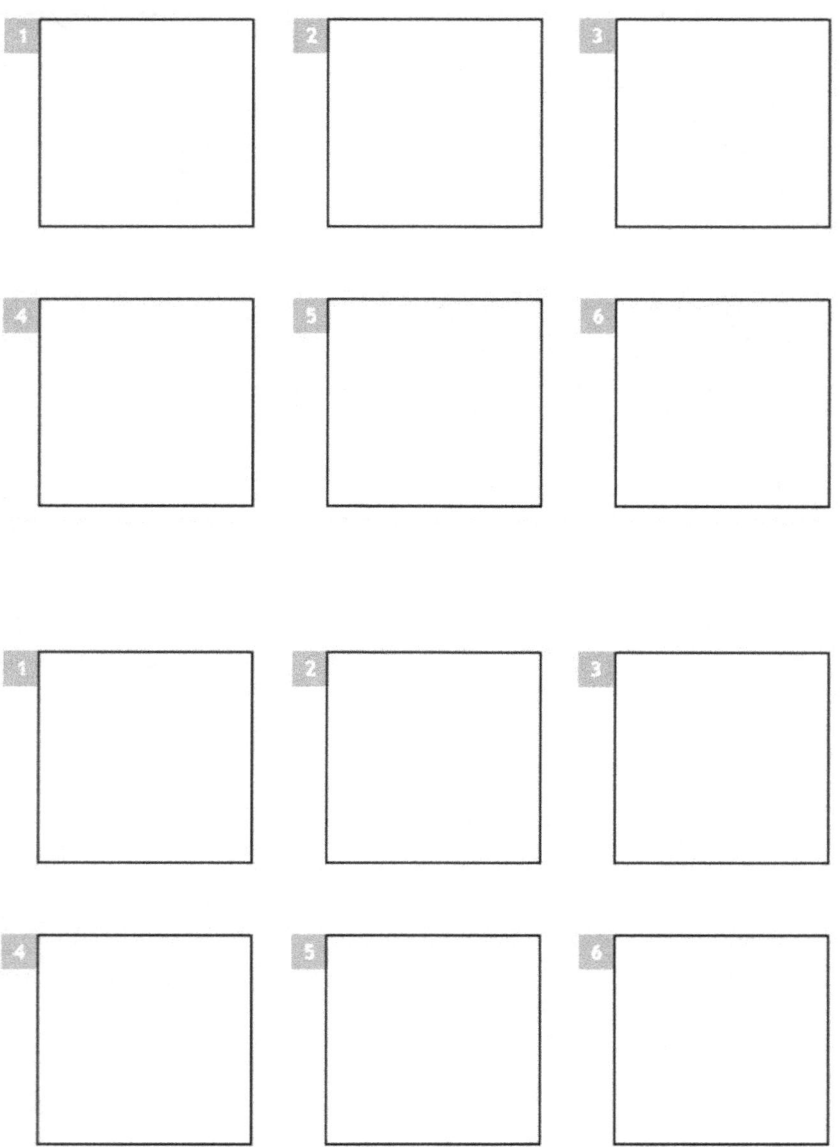

Make Your Own Doodle

Using the Pattern

Pattern #6: Printemps

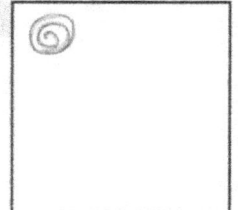 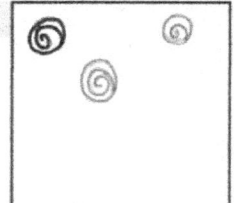 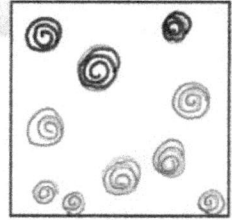

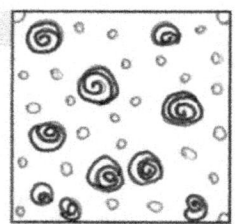 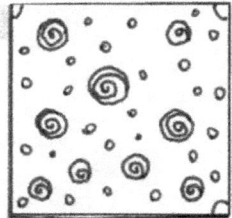

Practice the Steps Below

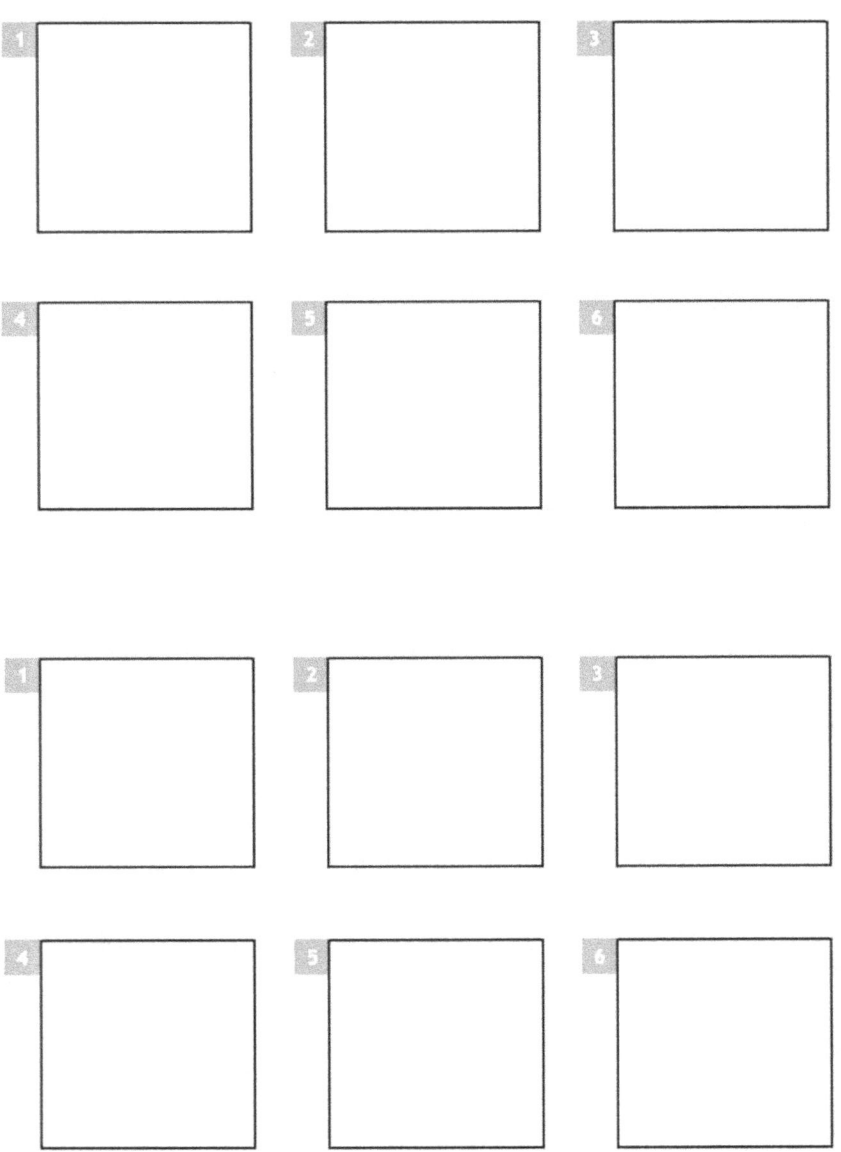

Make Your Own Doodle

Using the Pattern

Pattern #7: Fife

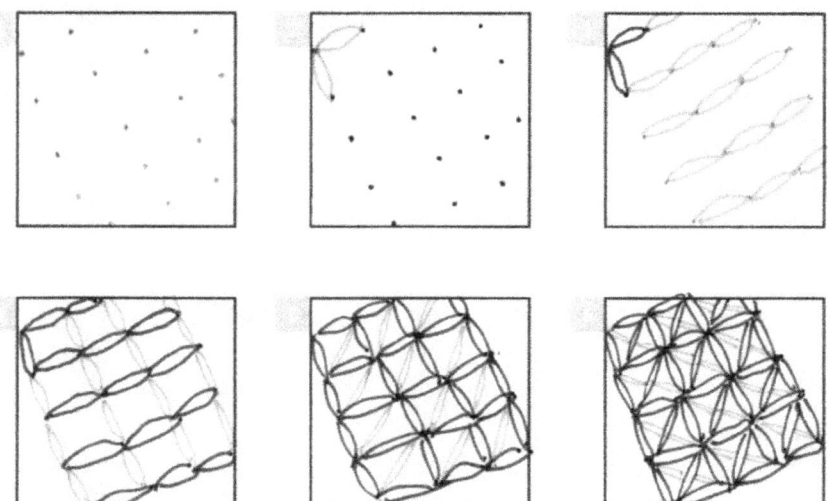

Practice the Steps Below

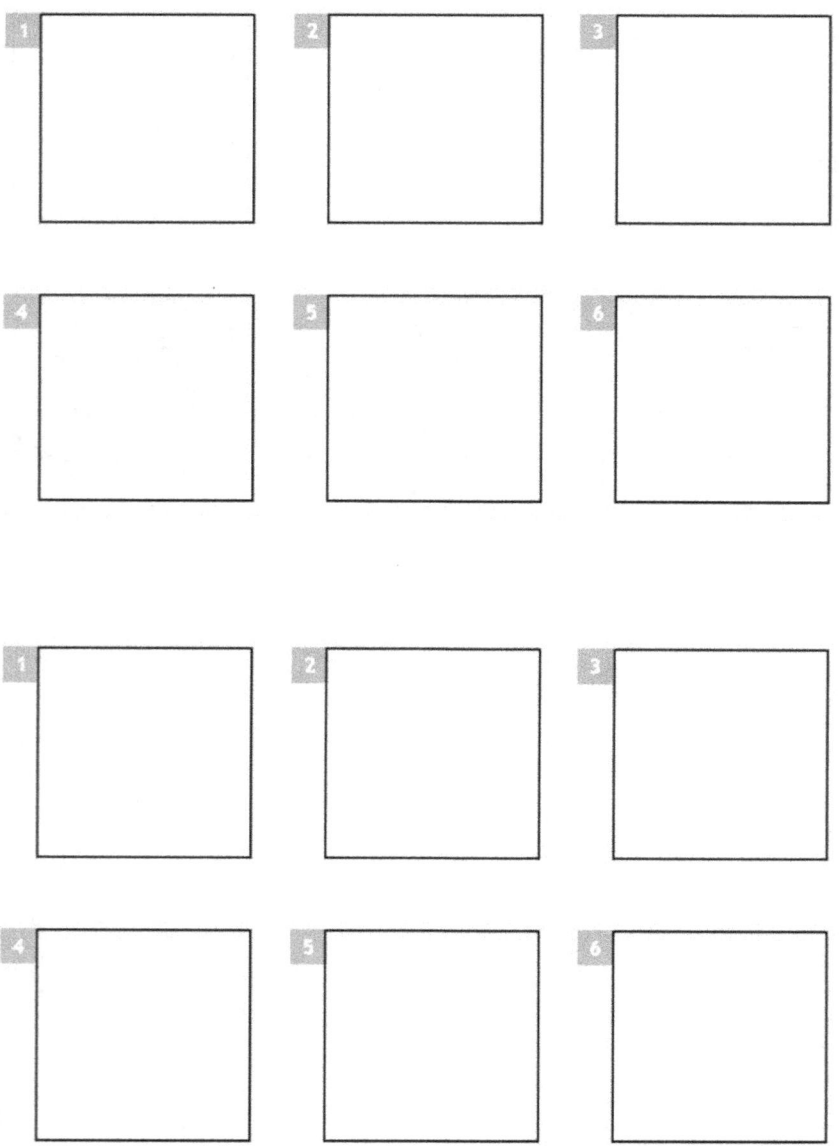

Make Your Own Doodle

Using the Pattern

Pattern #8: Jonqal

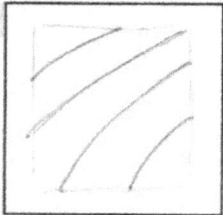 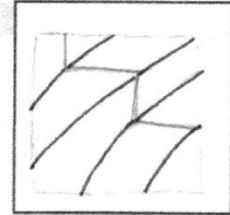 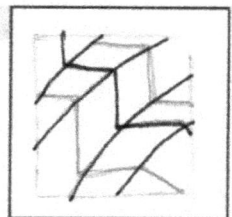

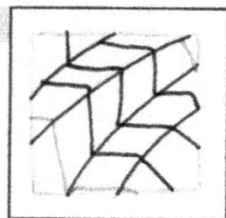 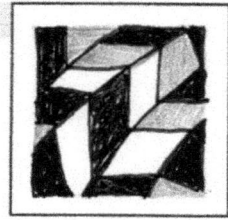

Practice the Steps Below

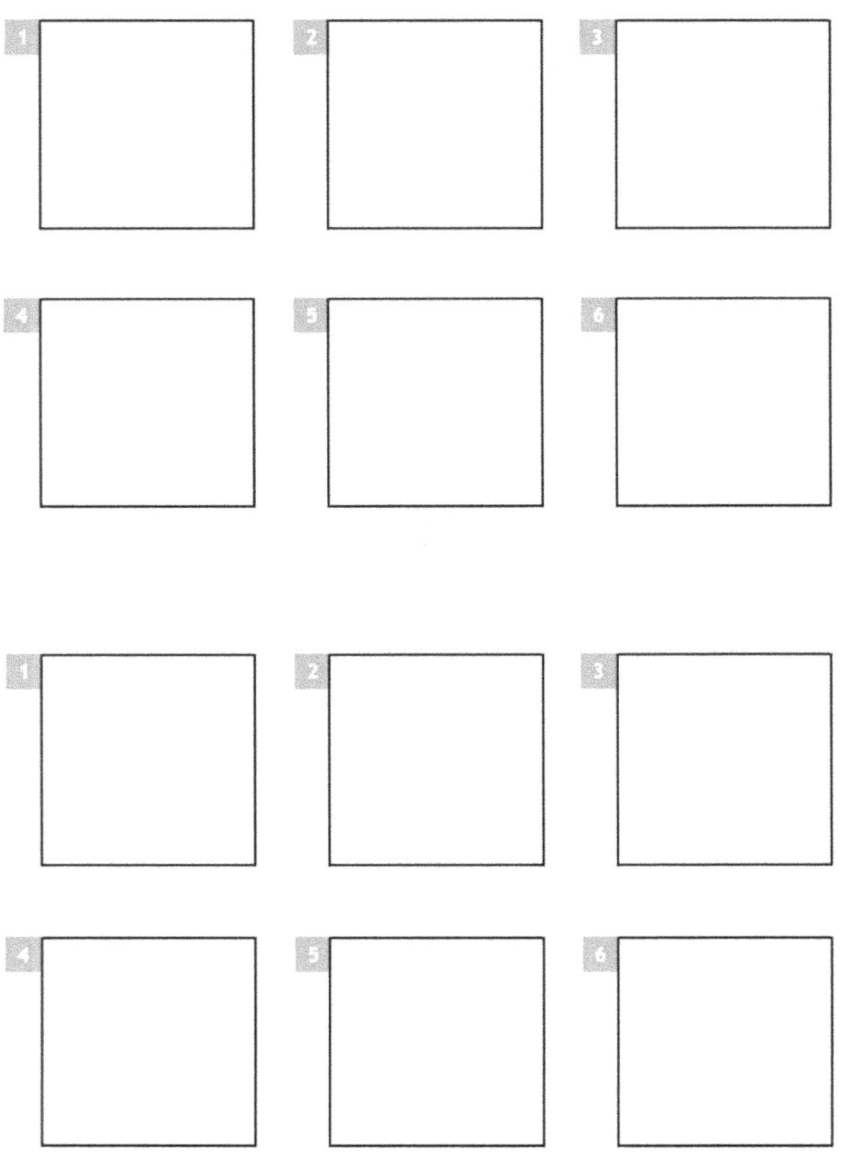

Make Your Own Doodle
Using the Pattern

Pattern #9: Emingle

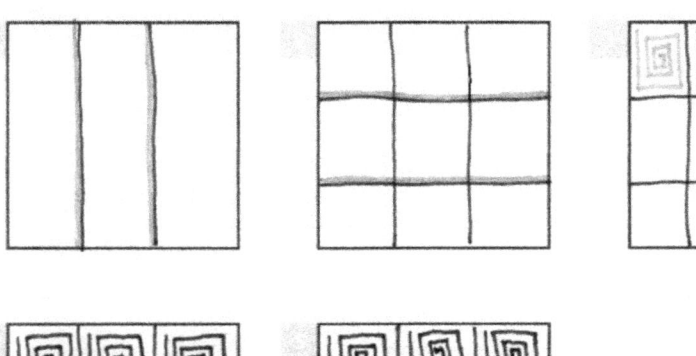

Practice the Steps Below

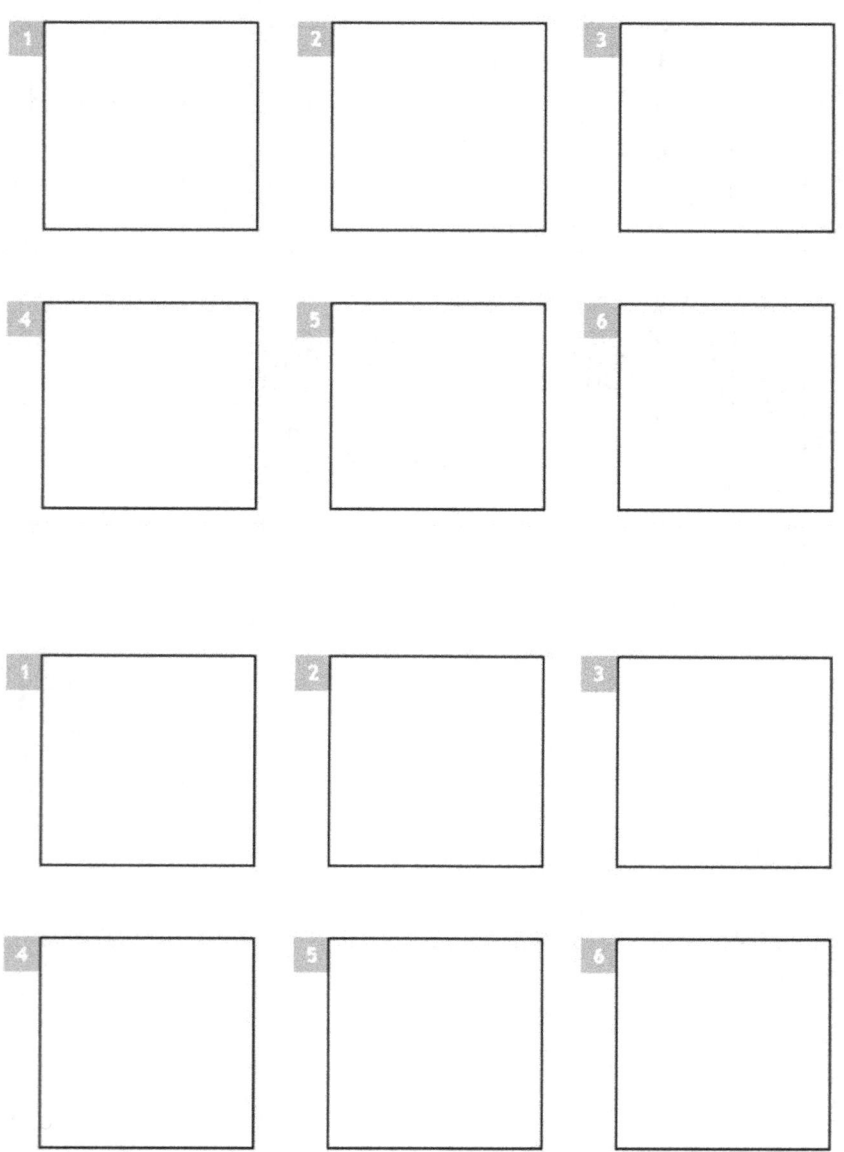

Make Your Own Doodle

Using the Pattern

Pattern #10: Pokeleaf

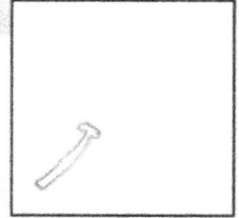
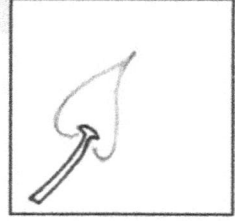
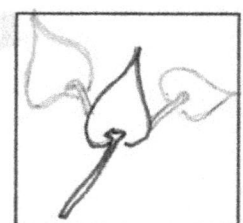

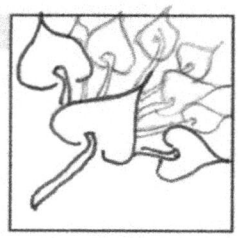
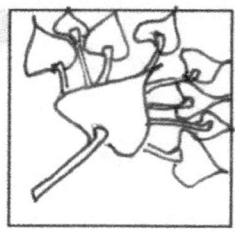

Practice the Steps Below

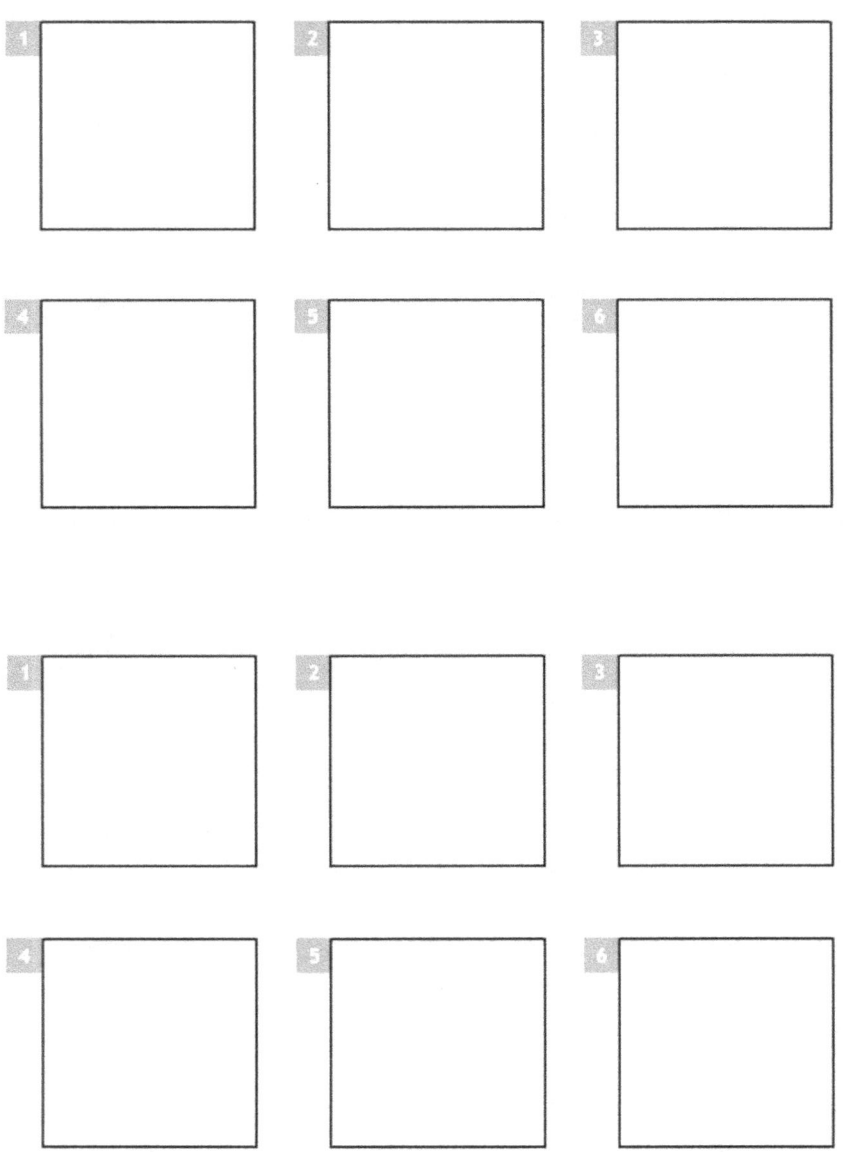

Make Your Own Doodle
Using the Pattern

Pattern #11: Finery

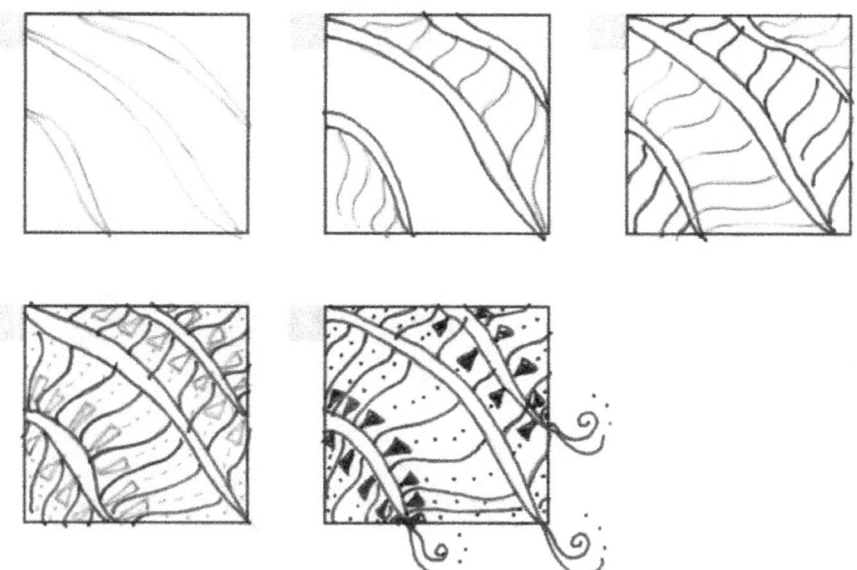

Practice the Steps Below

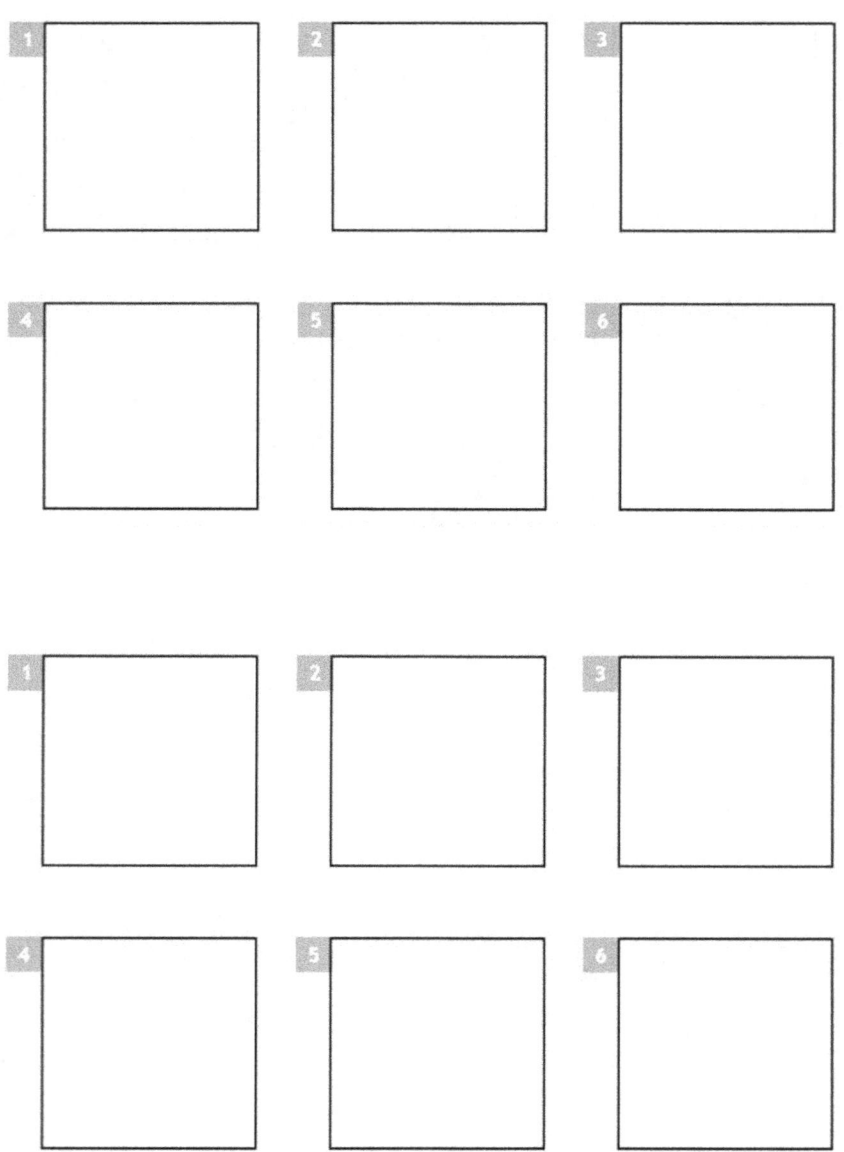

Make Your Own Doodle

Using the Pattern

Pattern #12: Mooka

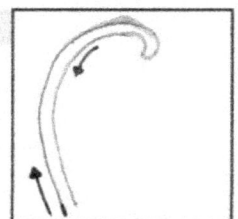 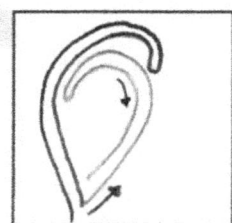 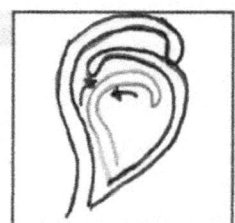

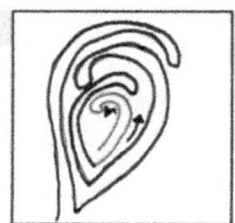 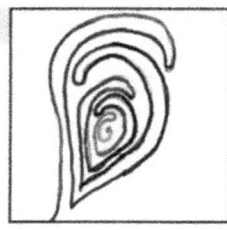

Practice the Steps Below

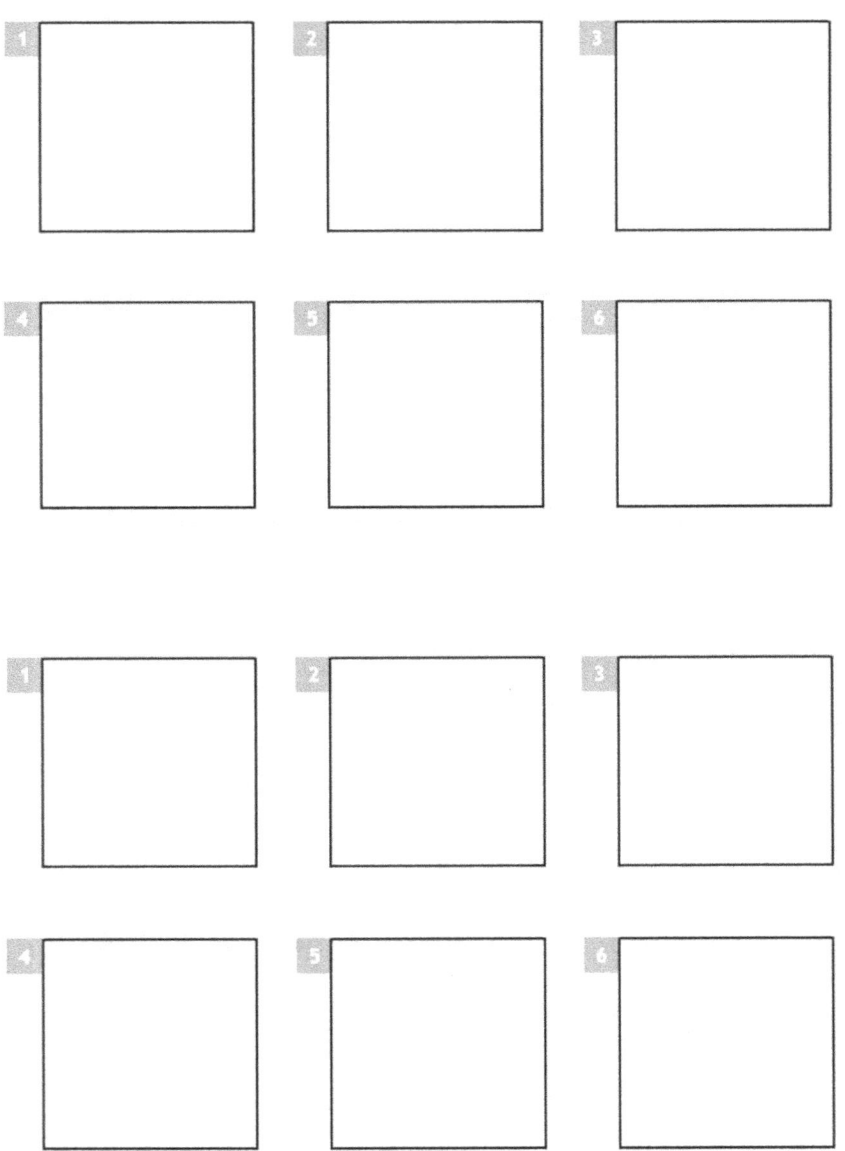

Make Your Own Doodle
Using the Pattern

Pattern #13: Verdigogh

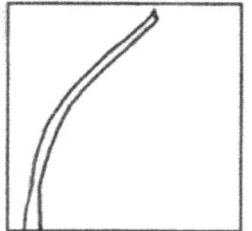 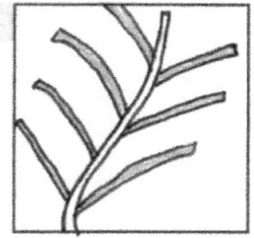 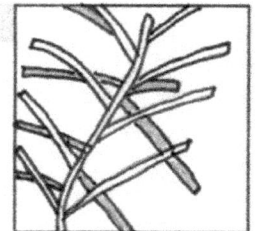

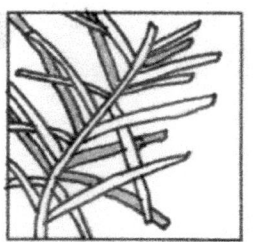 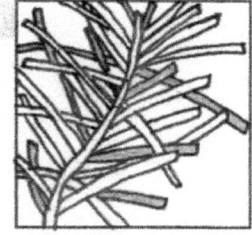

Practice the Steps Below

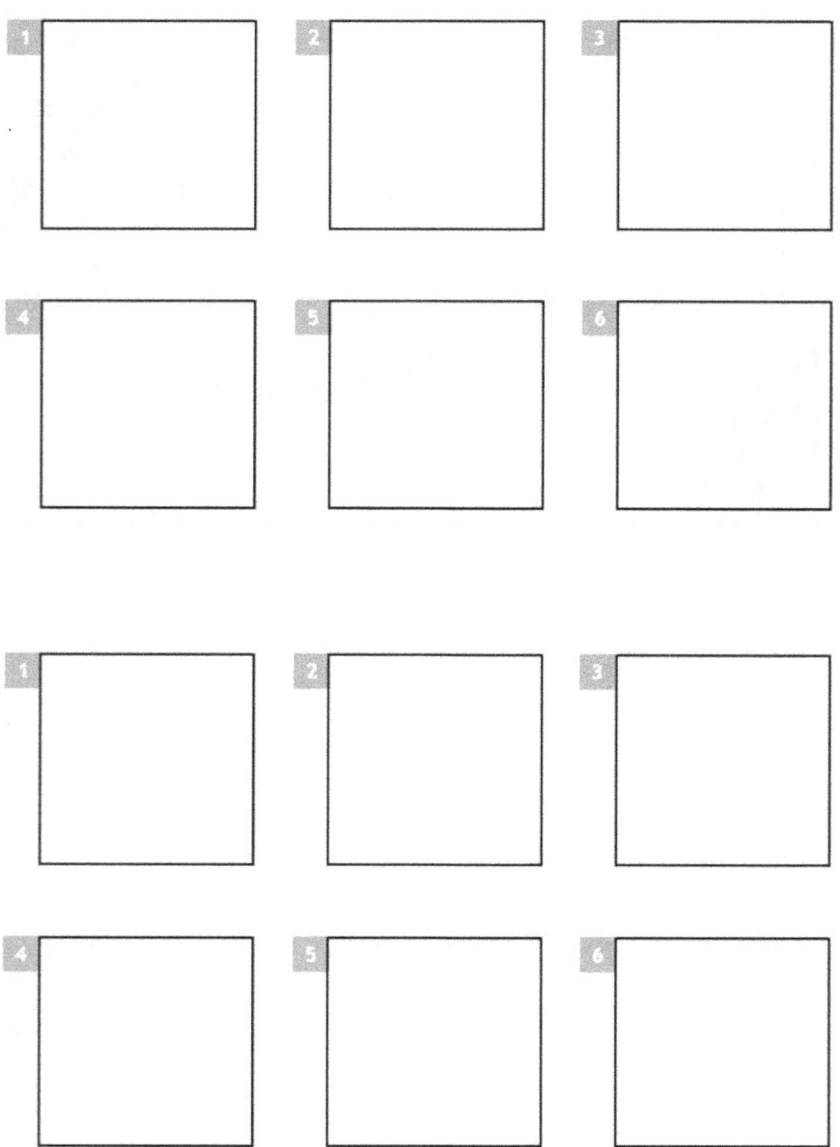

Make Your Own Doodle
Using the Pattern

Pattern #14: Tortuca

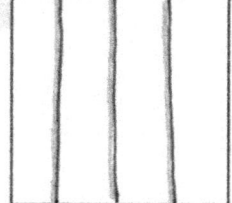 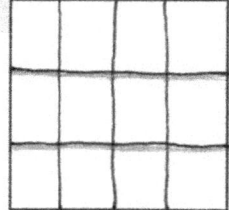 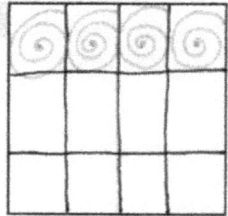

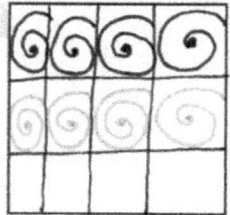 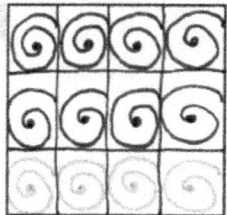

Practice the Steps Below

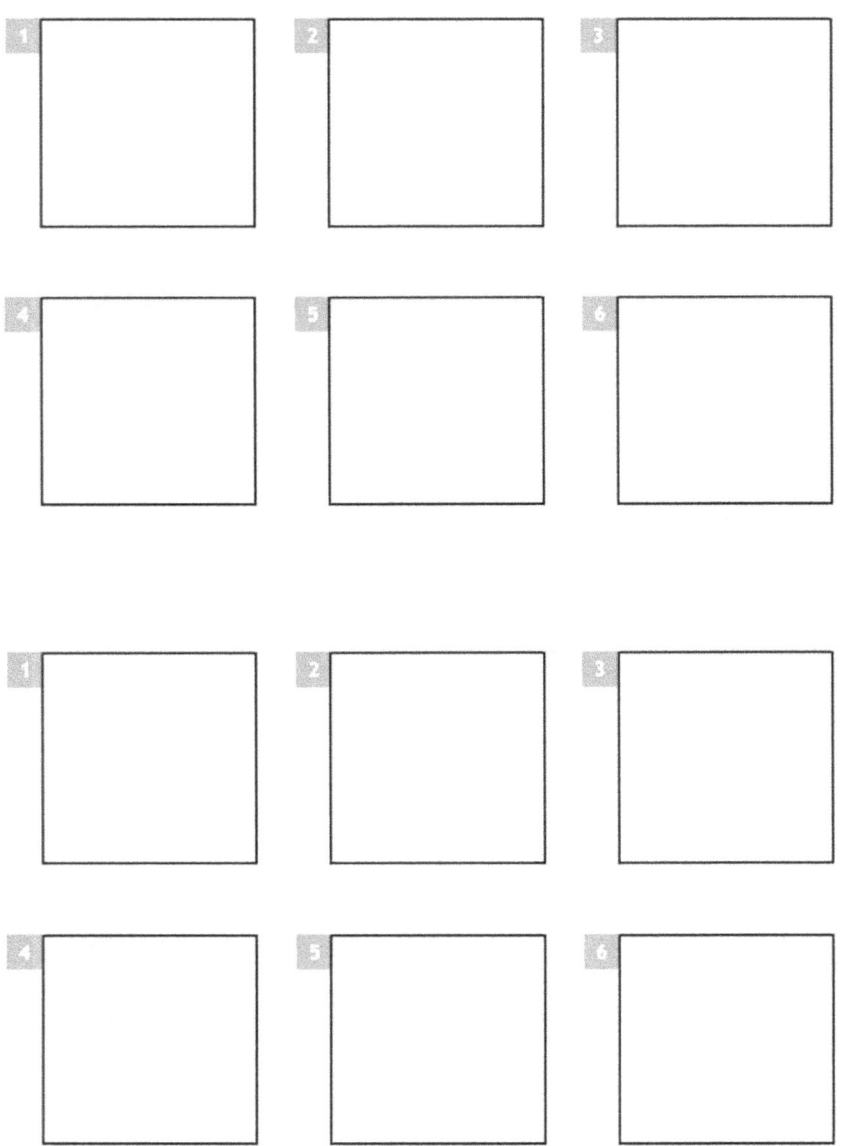

Make Your Own Doodle
Using the Pattern

Pattern #15: Bronx Cheer

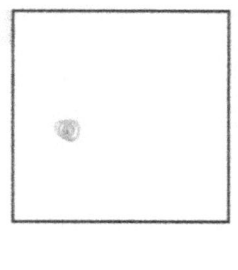 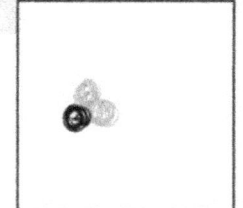 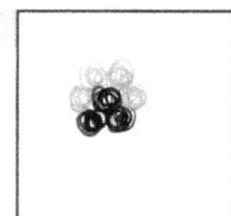

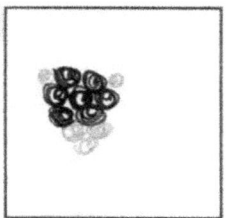 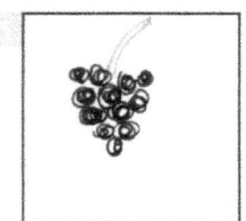 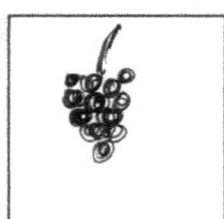

Practice the Steps Below

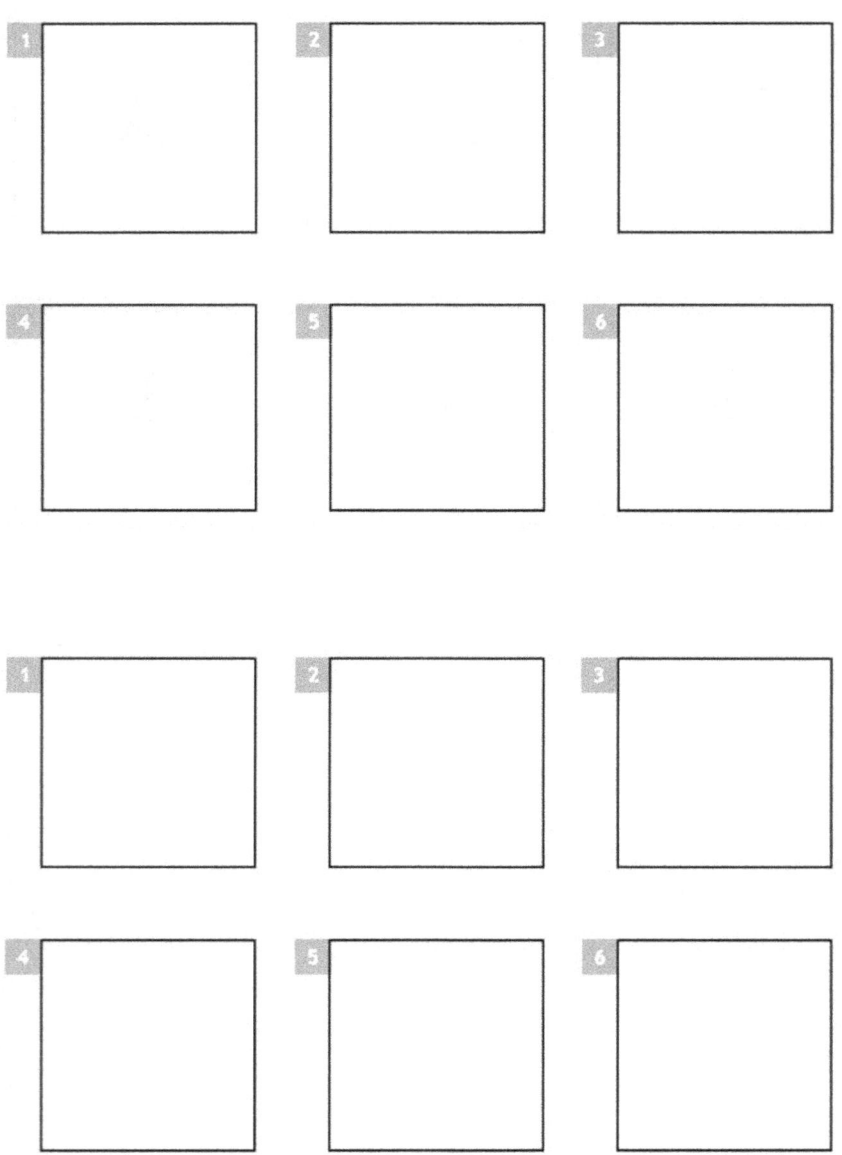

Make Your Own Doodle

Using the Pattern

Pattern #16: Cadent

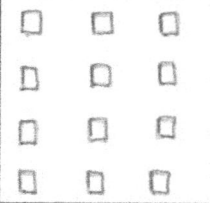 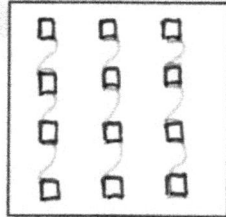 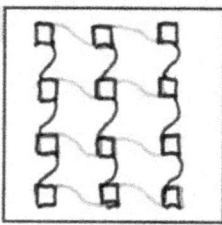

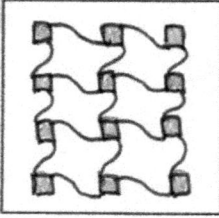 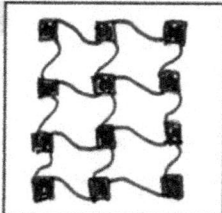

Practice the Steps Below

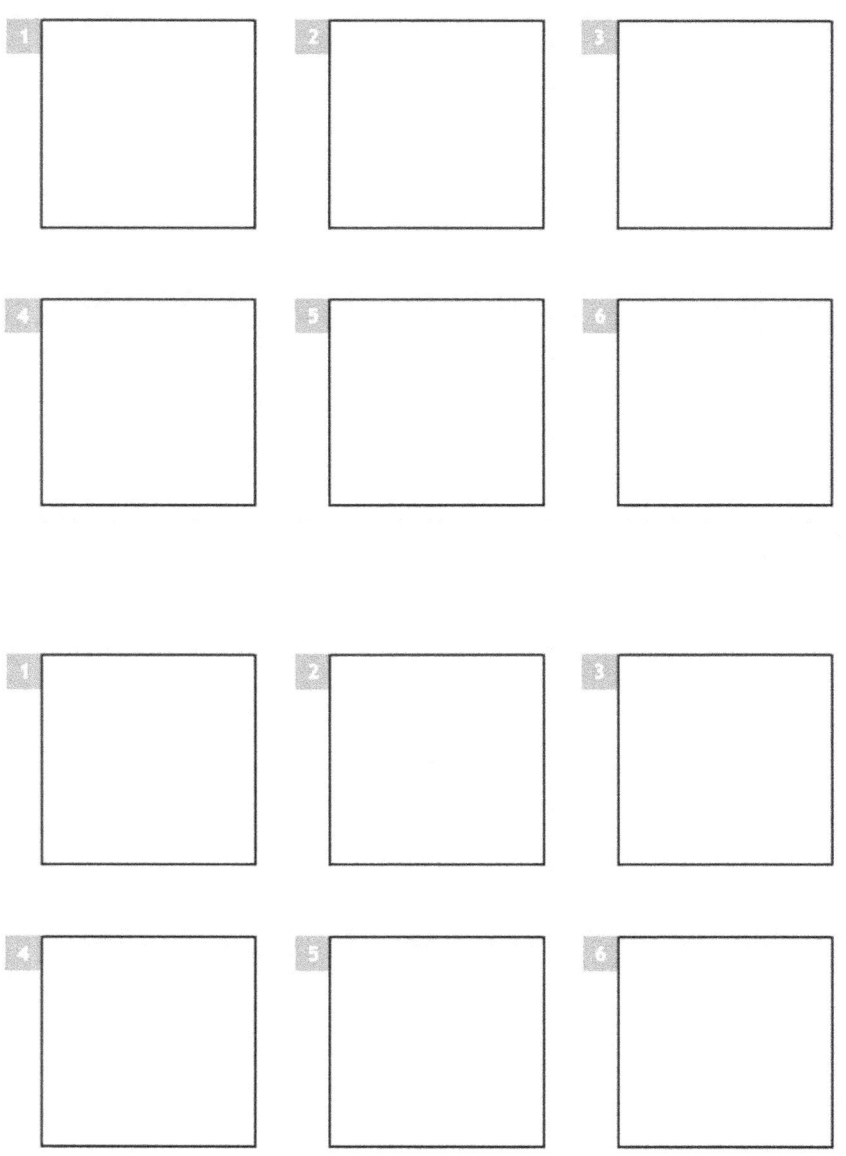

Make Your Own Doodle
Using the Pattern

Pattern #17: Schway

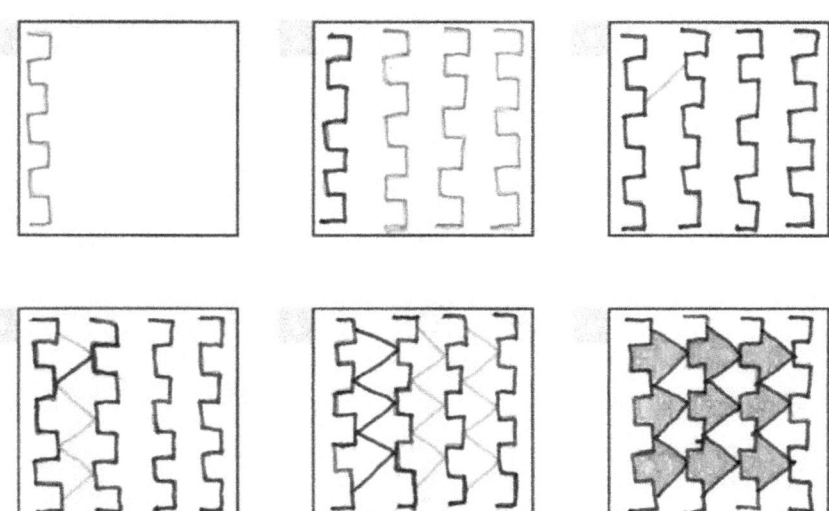

Practice the Steps Below

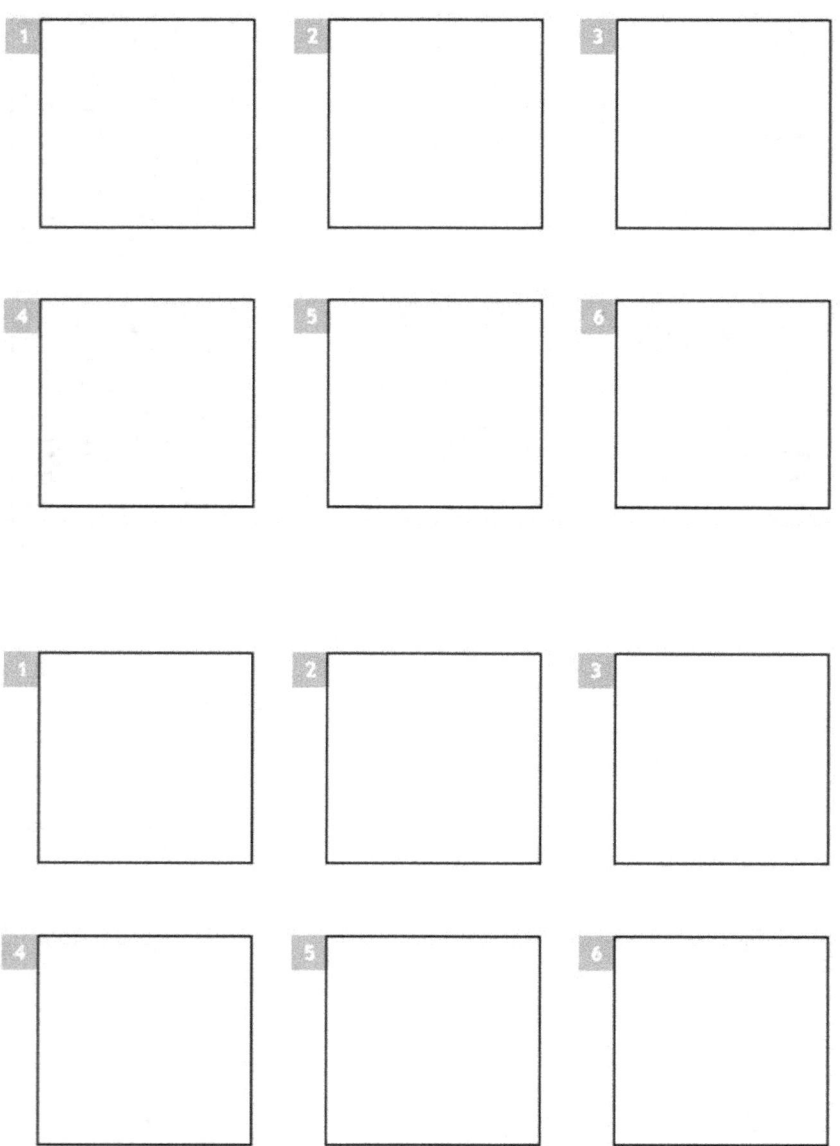

Make Your Own Doodle
Using the Pattern

Pattern #18: Crescent Moon

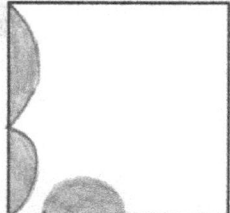 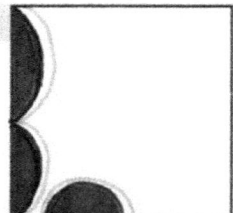 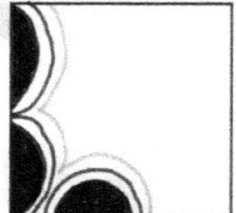

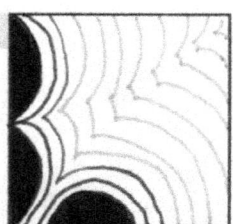 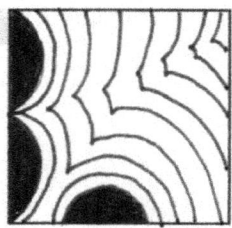

Practice the Steps Below

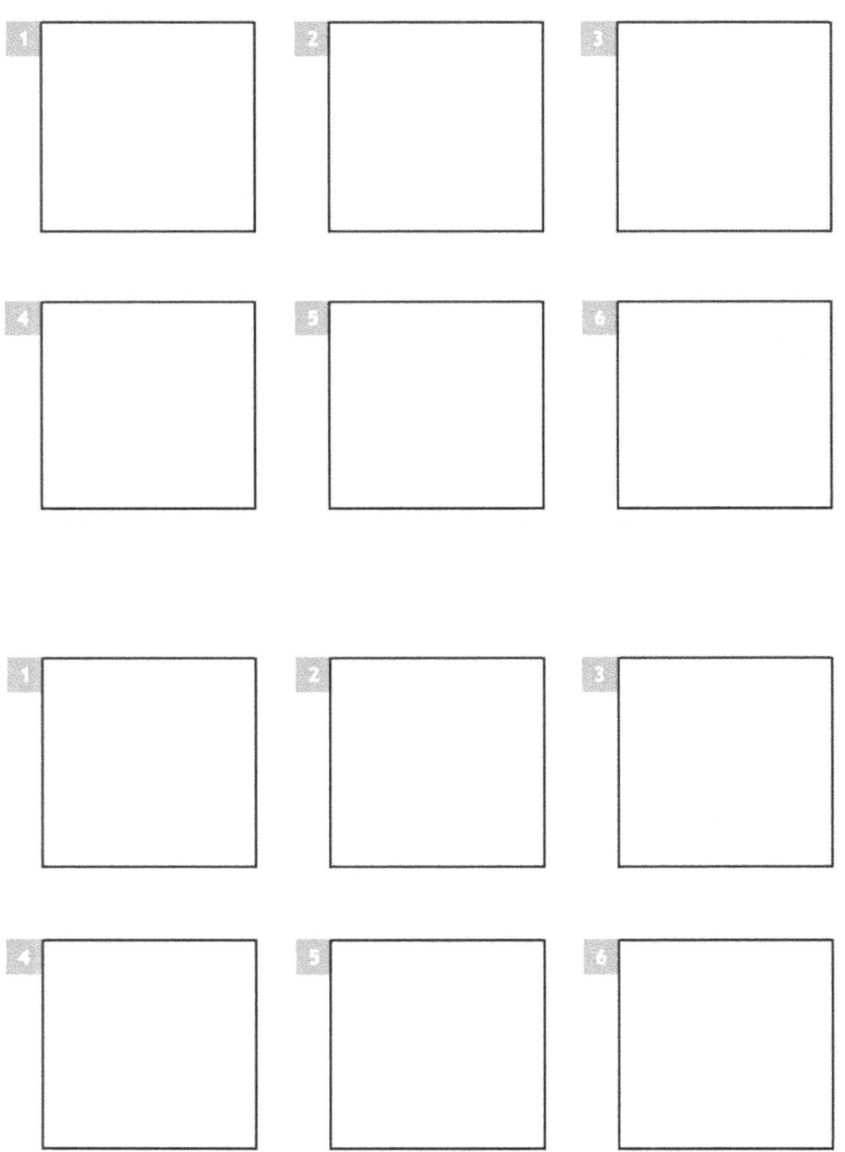

Make Your Own Doodle

Using the Pattern

Pattern #19: Quib

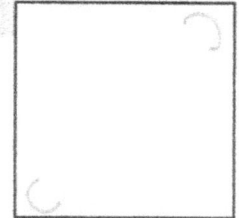 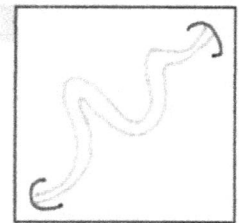 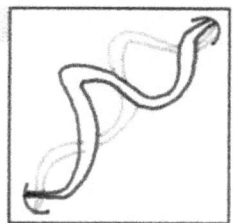

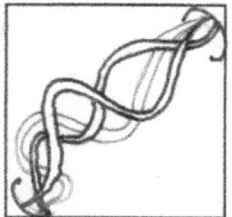 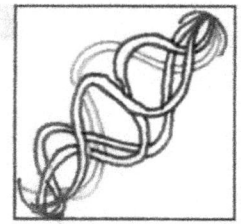 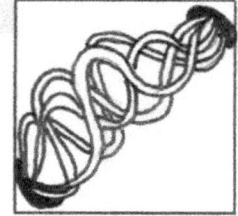

Practice the Steps Below

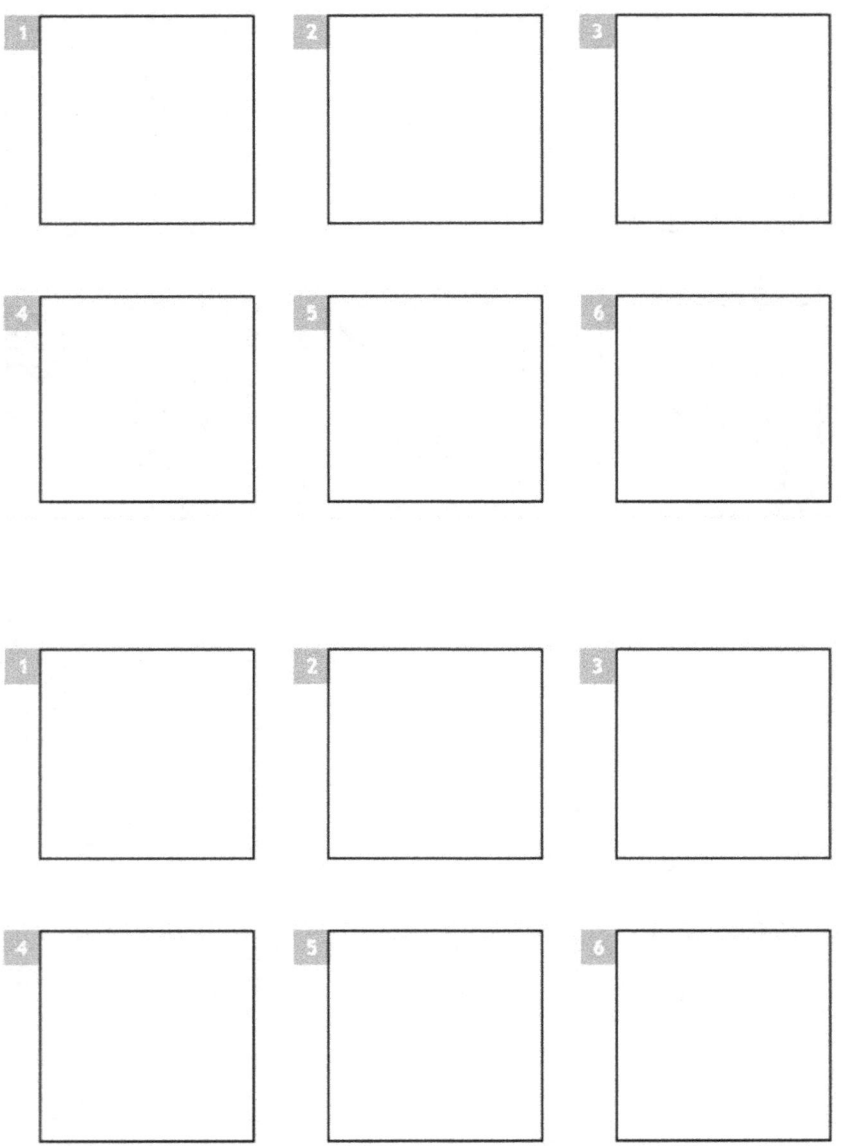

Make Your Own Doodle
Using the Pattern

Pattern #20: Chainging

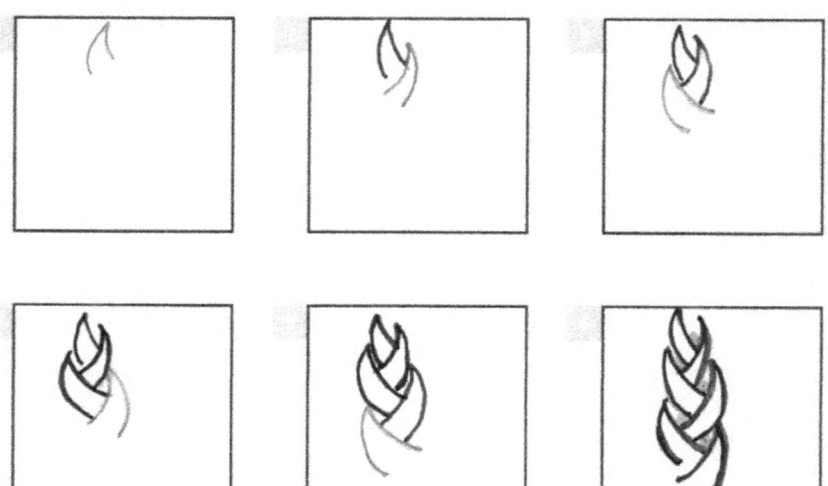

Practice the Steps Below

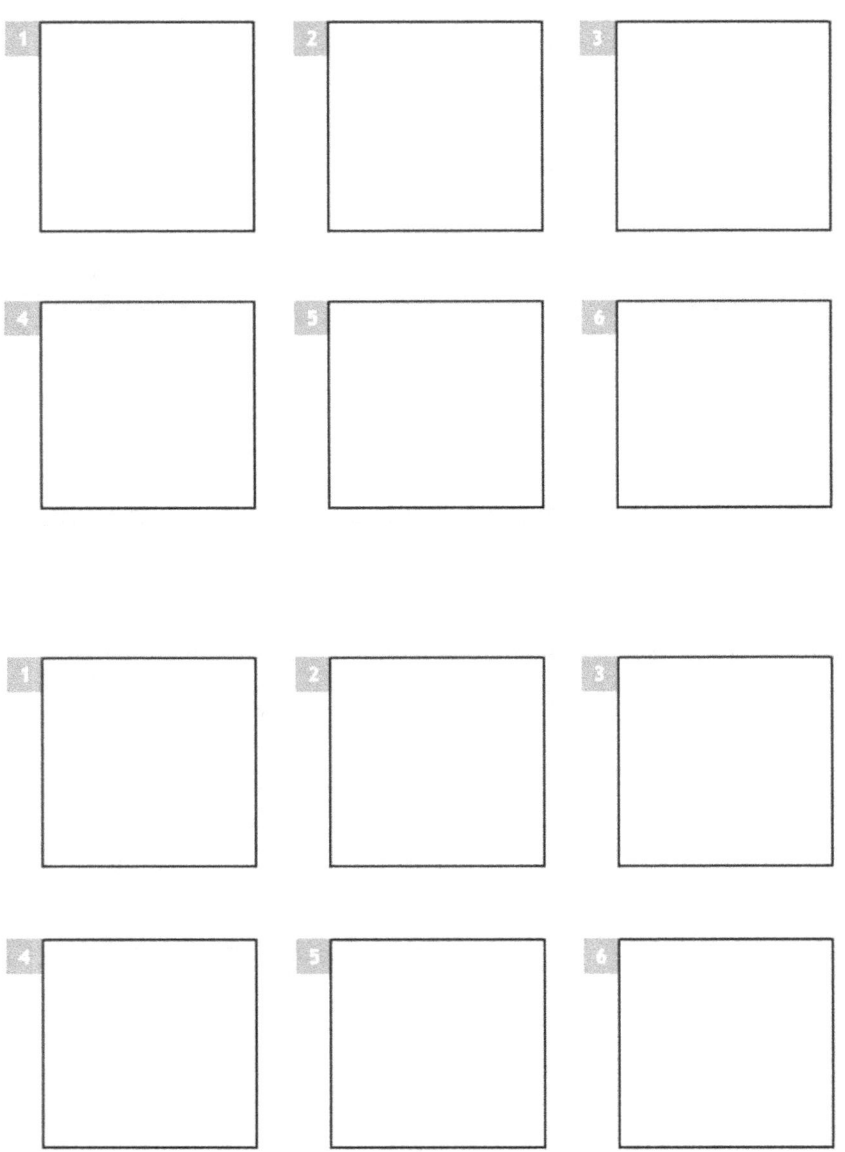

Make Your Own Doodle

Using the Pattern

Pattern #21: Cirquital

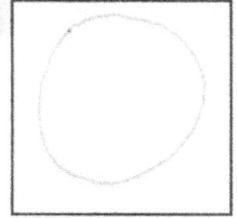 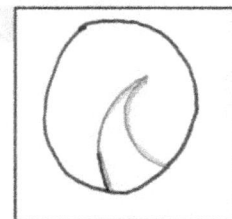 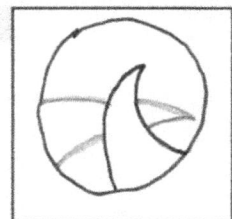

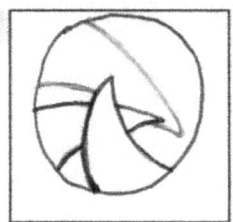 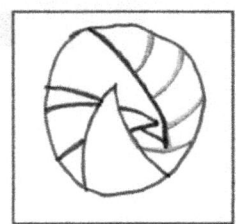 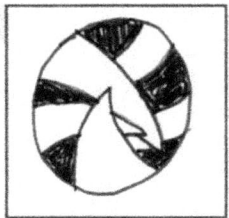

Practice the Steps Below

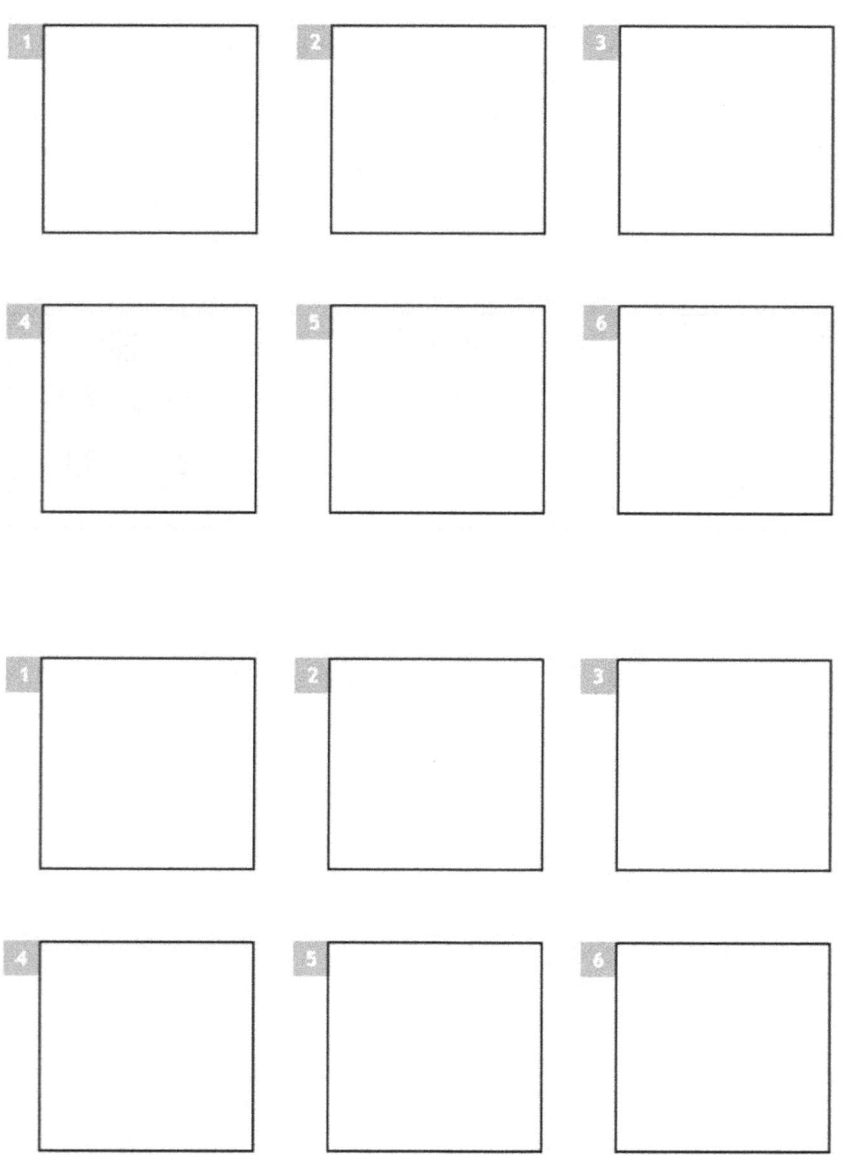

Make Your Own Doodle

Using the Pattern

Pattern #22: Ynix

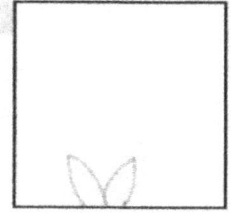 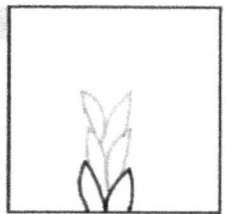 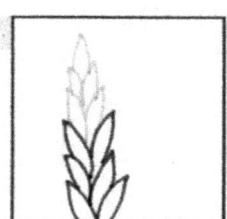

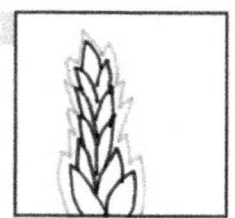 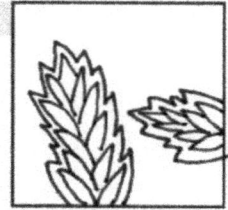

Practice the Steps Below

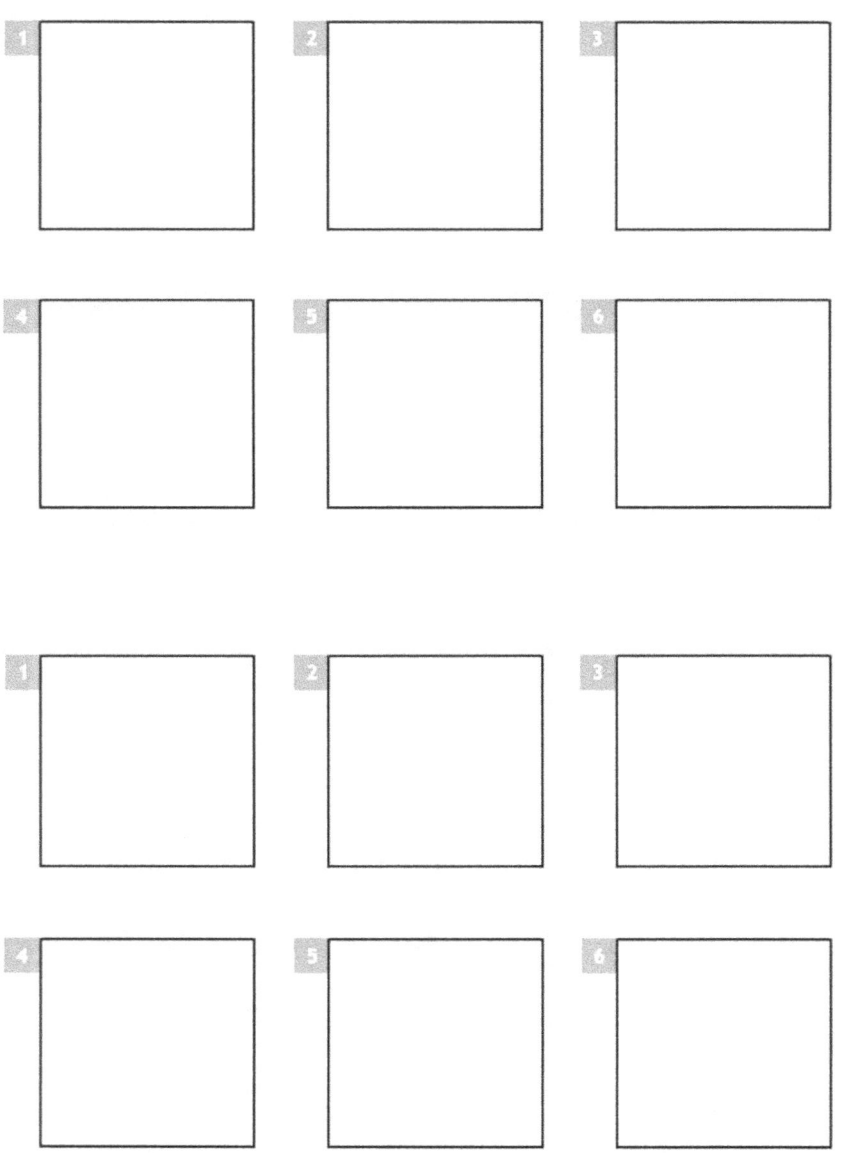

Make Your Own Doodle

Using the Pattern

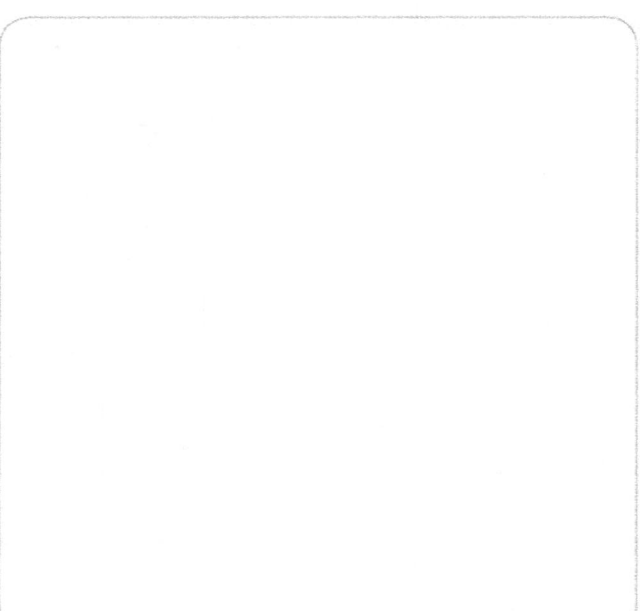

Pattern #23: Tidal

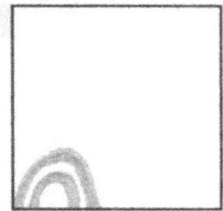 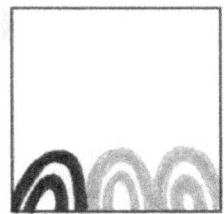 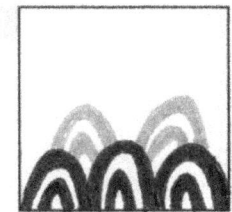

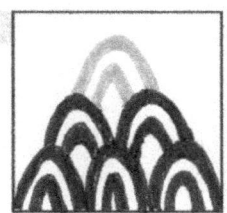 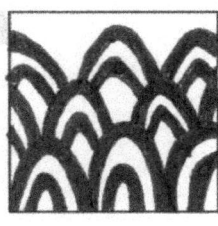

Practice the Steps Below

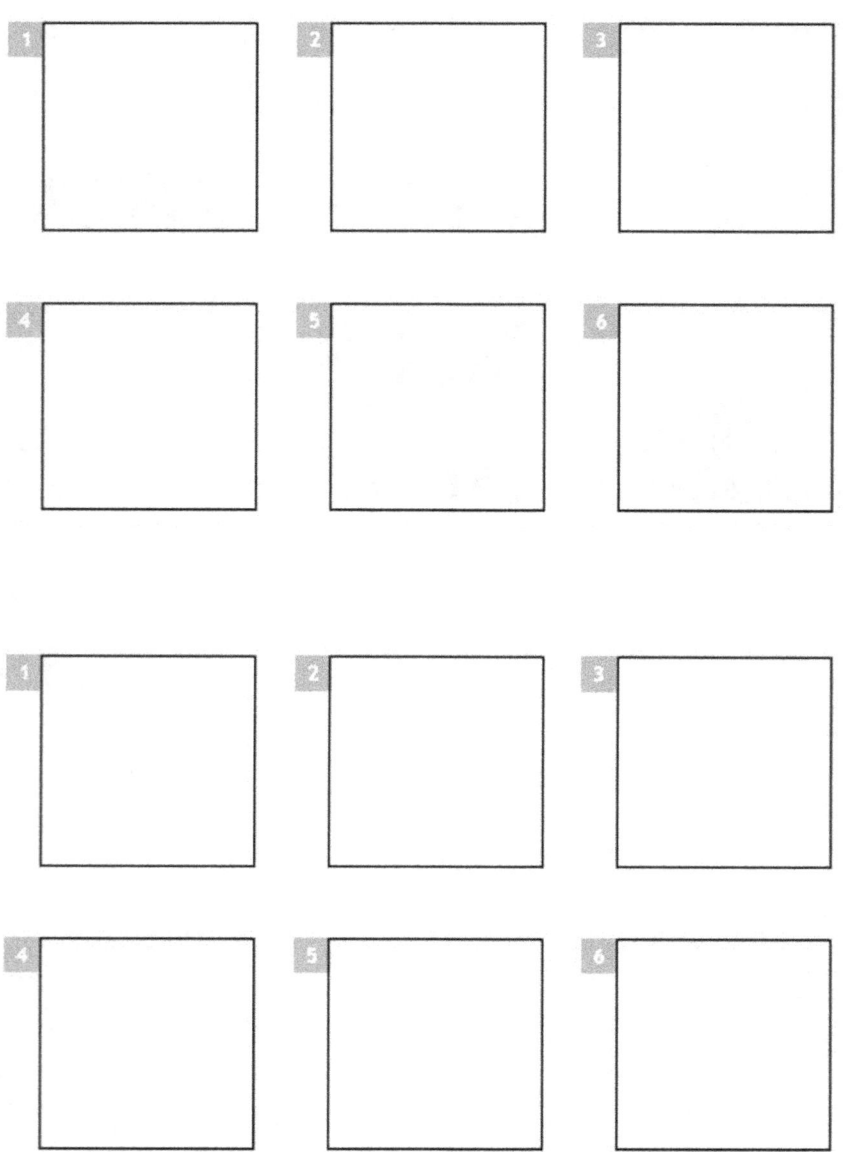

Make Your Own Doodle

Using the Pattern

Pattern #24: Flukes

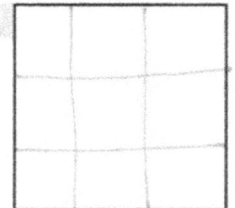 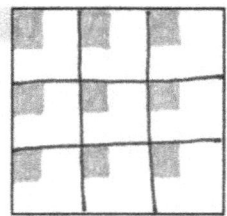 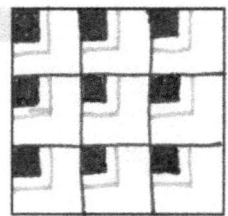

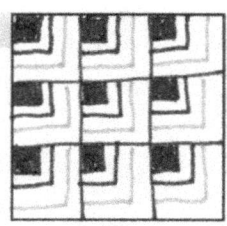 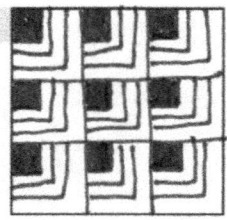

Practice the Steps Below

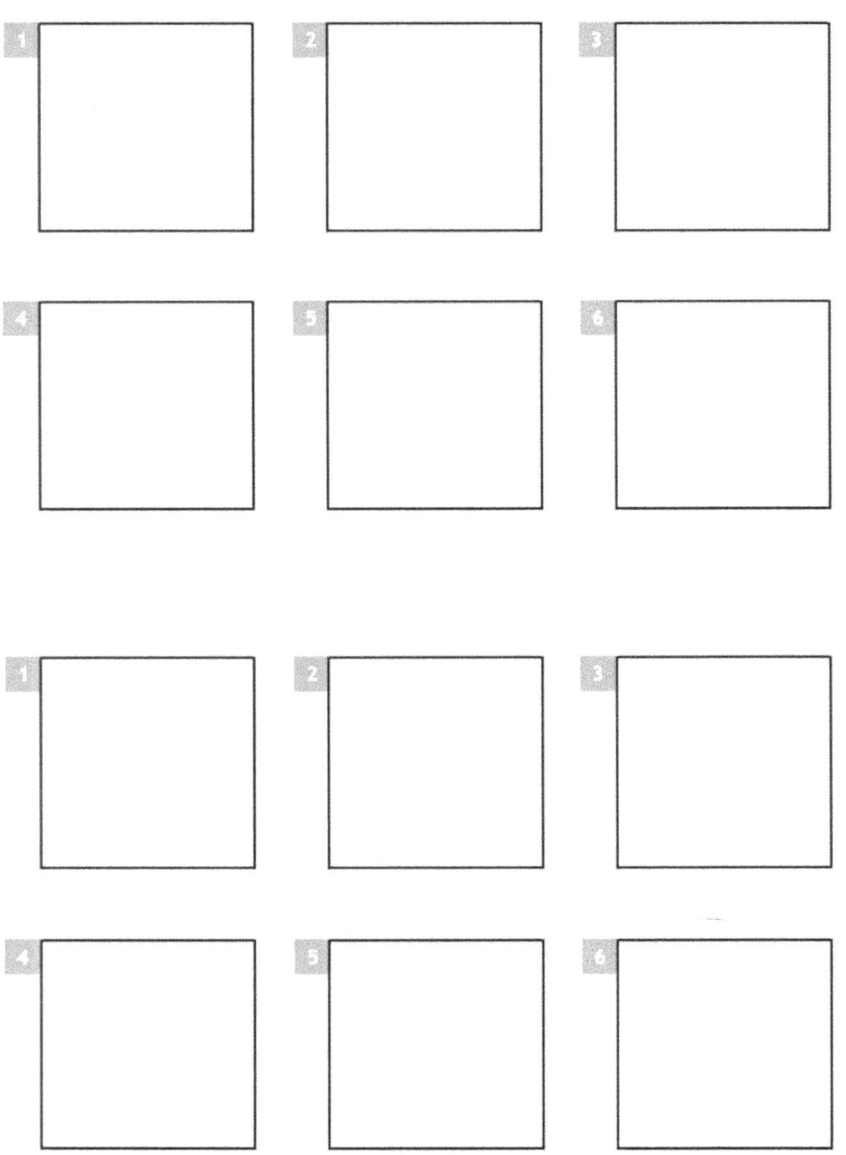

Make Your Own Doodle
Using the Pattern

Pattern #25: Floo

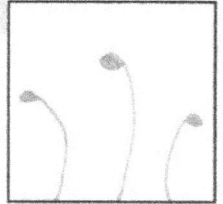 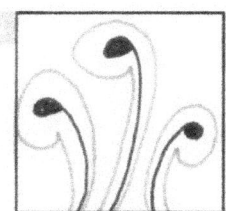 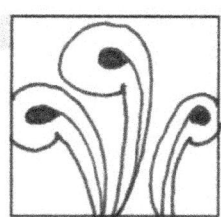

Practice the Steps Below

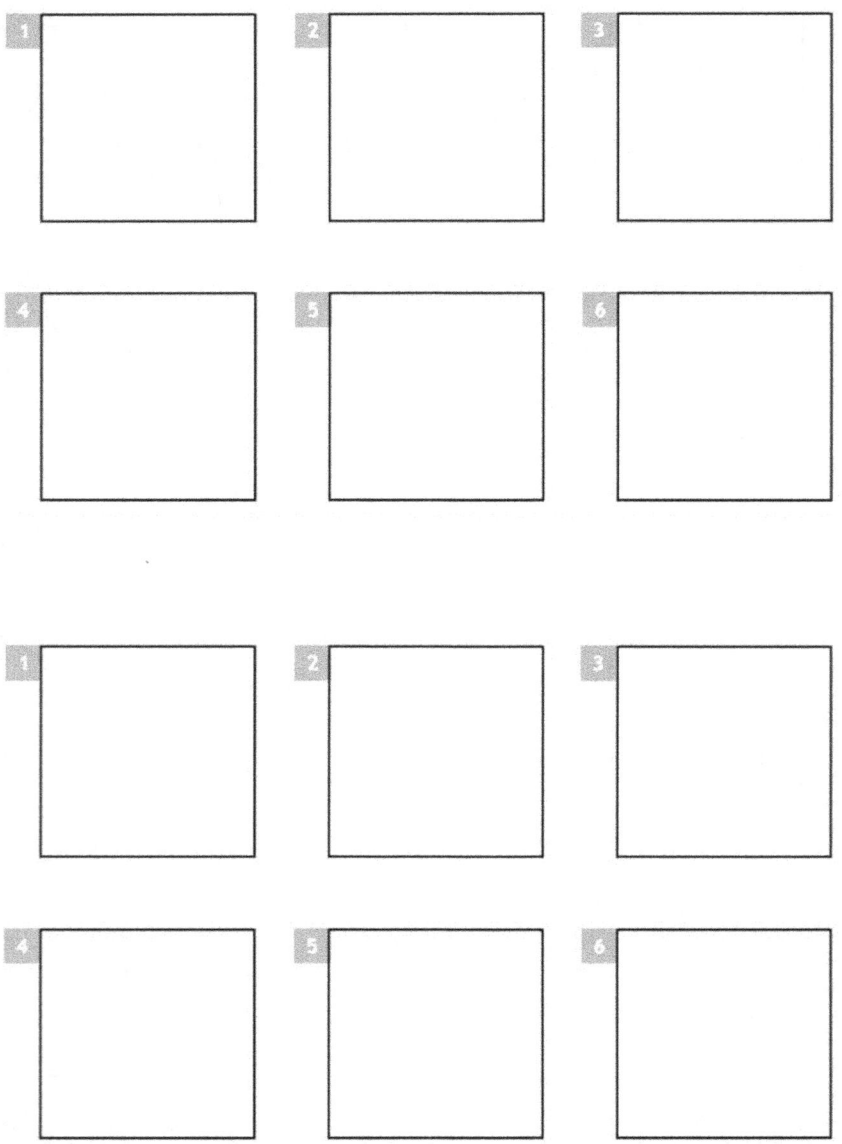

Make Your Own Doodle

Using the Pattern

Pattern #26: Vega

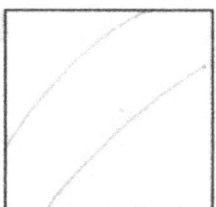 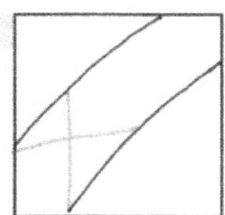 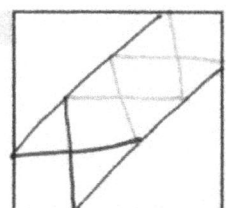

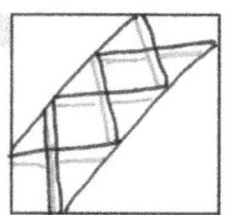 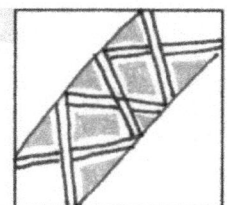 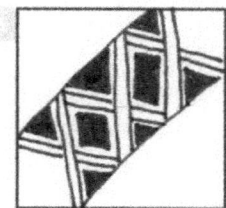

Practice the Steps Below

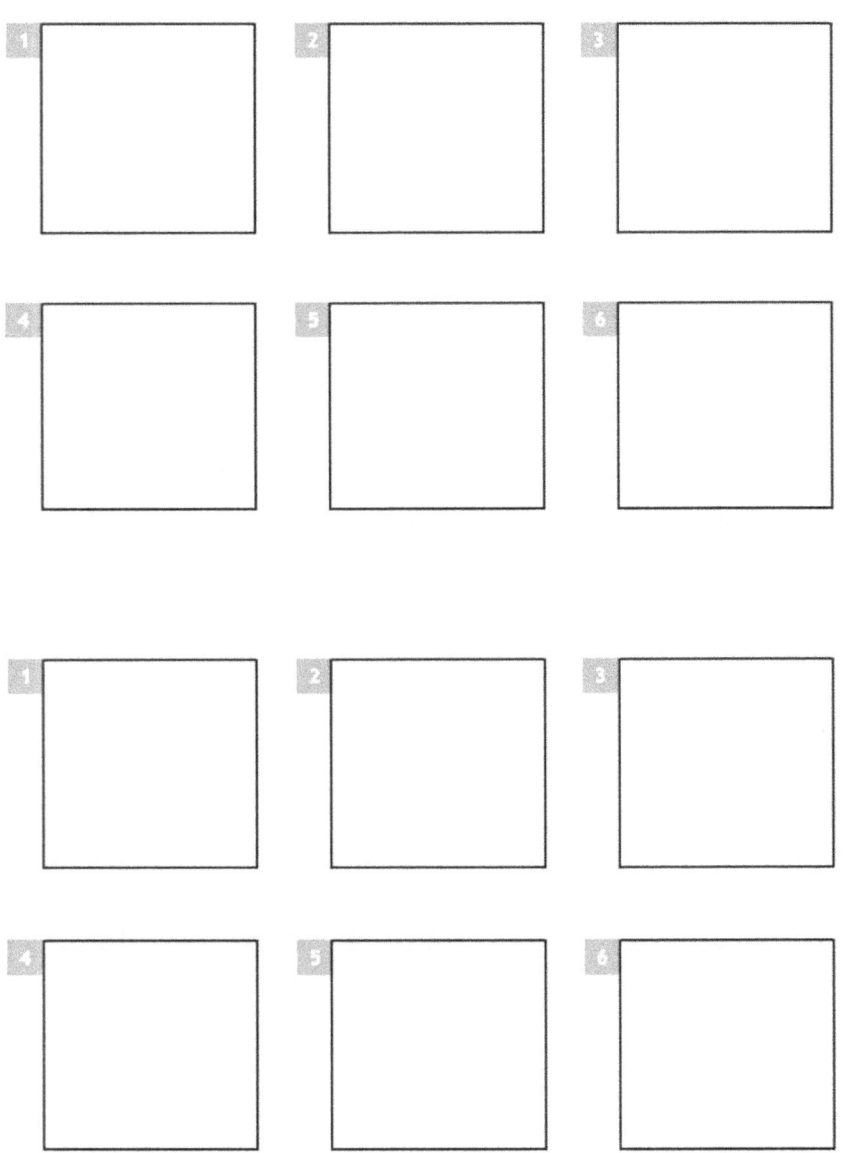

Make Your Own Doodle
Using the Pattern

Pattern #27: Enyshou

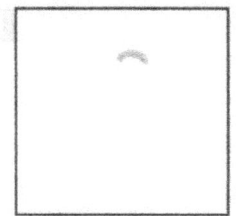 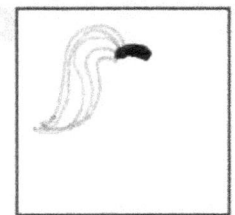 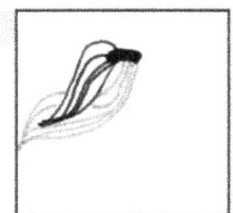

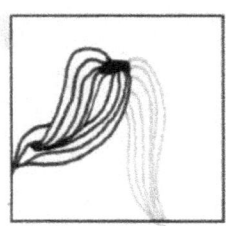 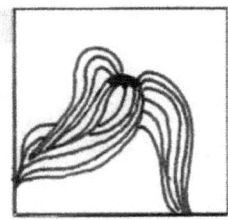

Practice the Steps Below

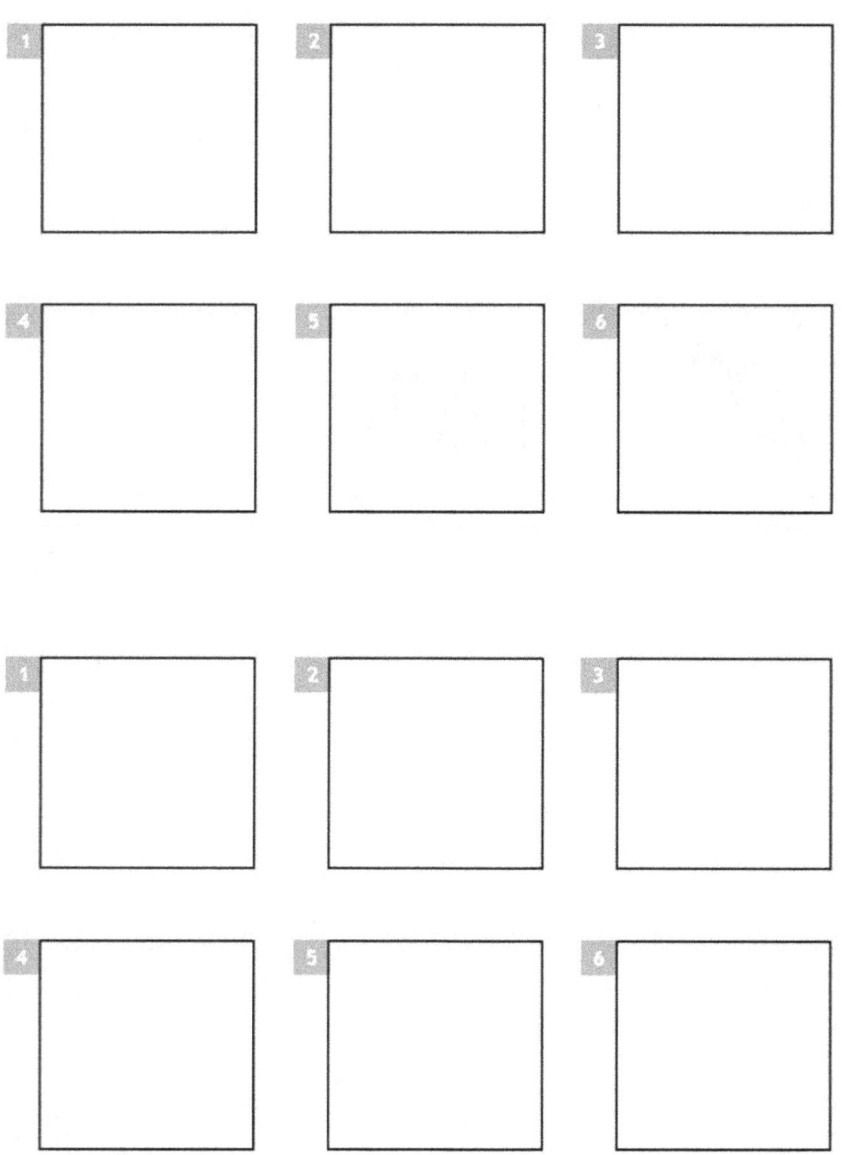

Make Your Own Doodle

Using the Pattern

Pattern #28: Static

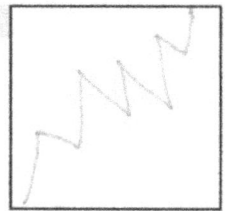 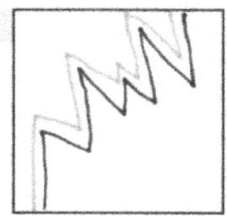 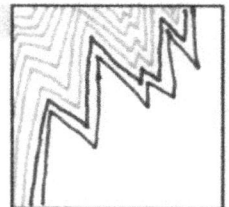

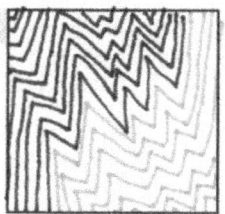 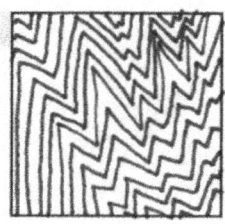

Practice the Steps Below

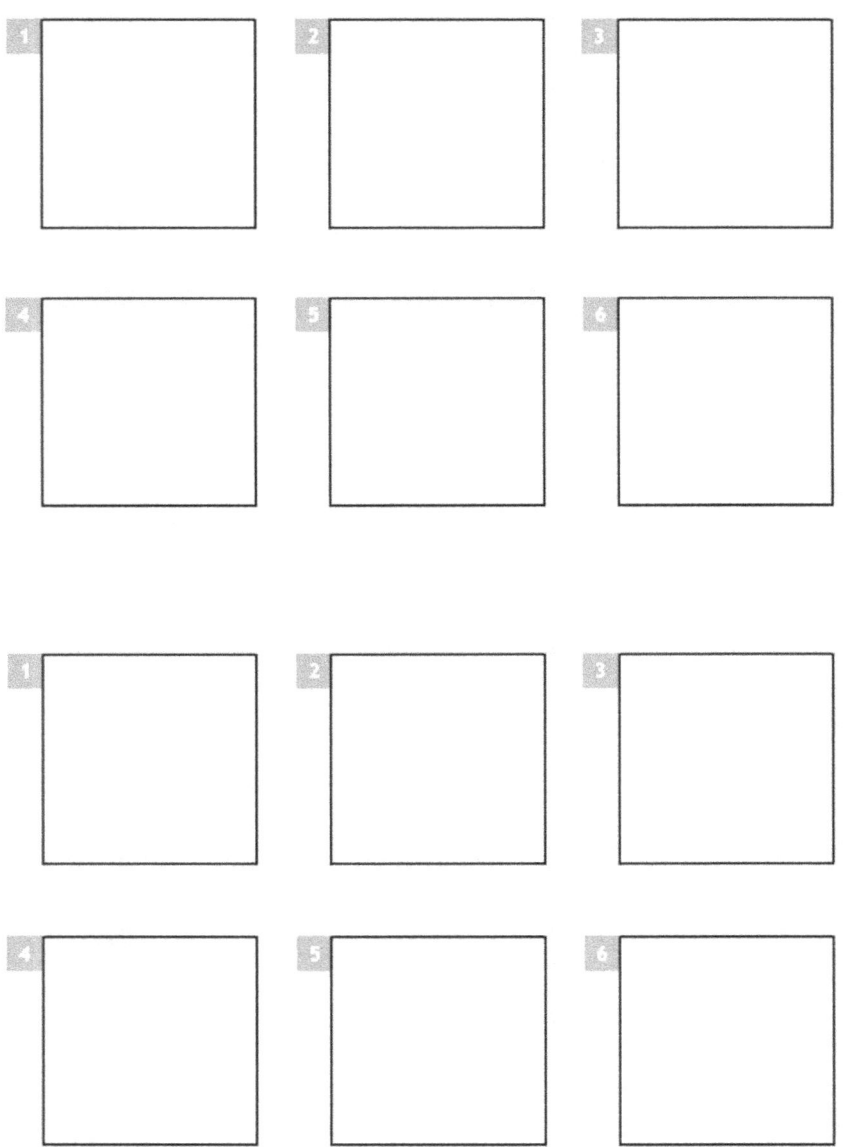

Make Your Own Doodle
Using the Pattern

Pattern #29: Cubine

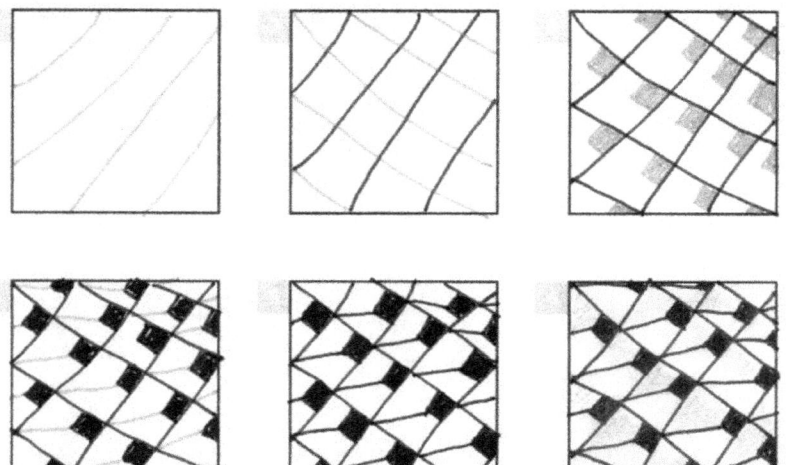

Practice the Steps Below

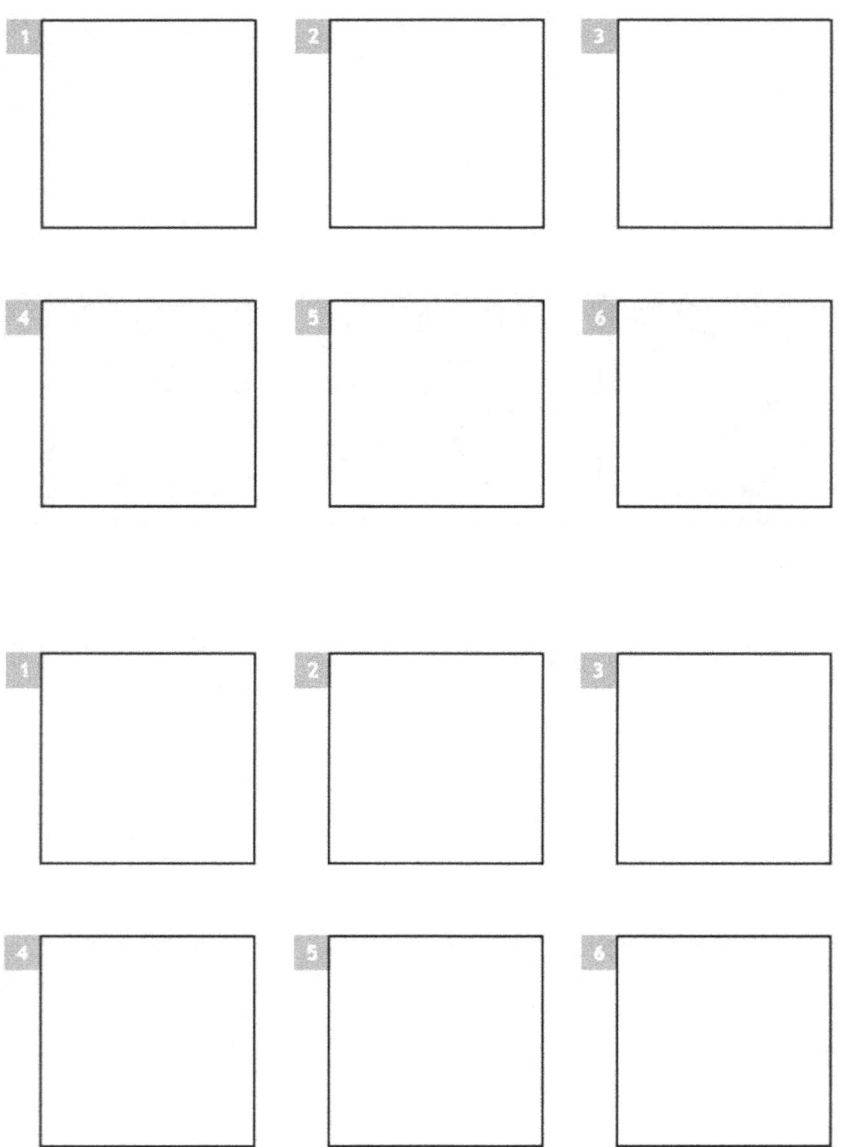

Make Your Own Doodle

Using the Pattern

Pattern #30: Msst

 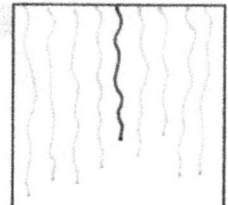 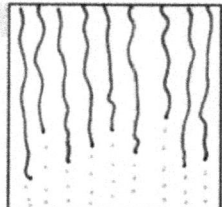

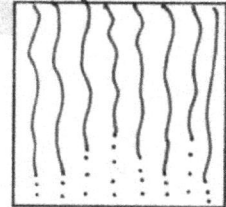

Practice the Steps Below

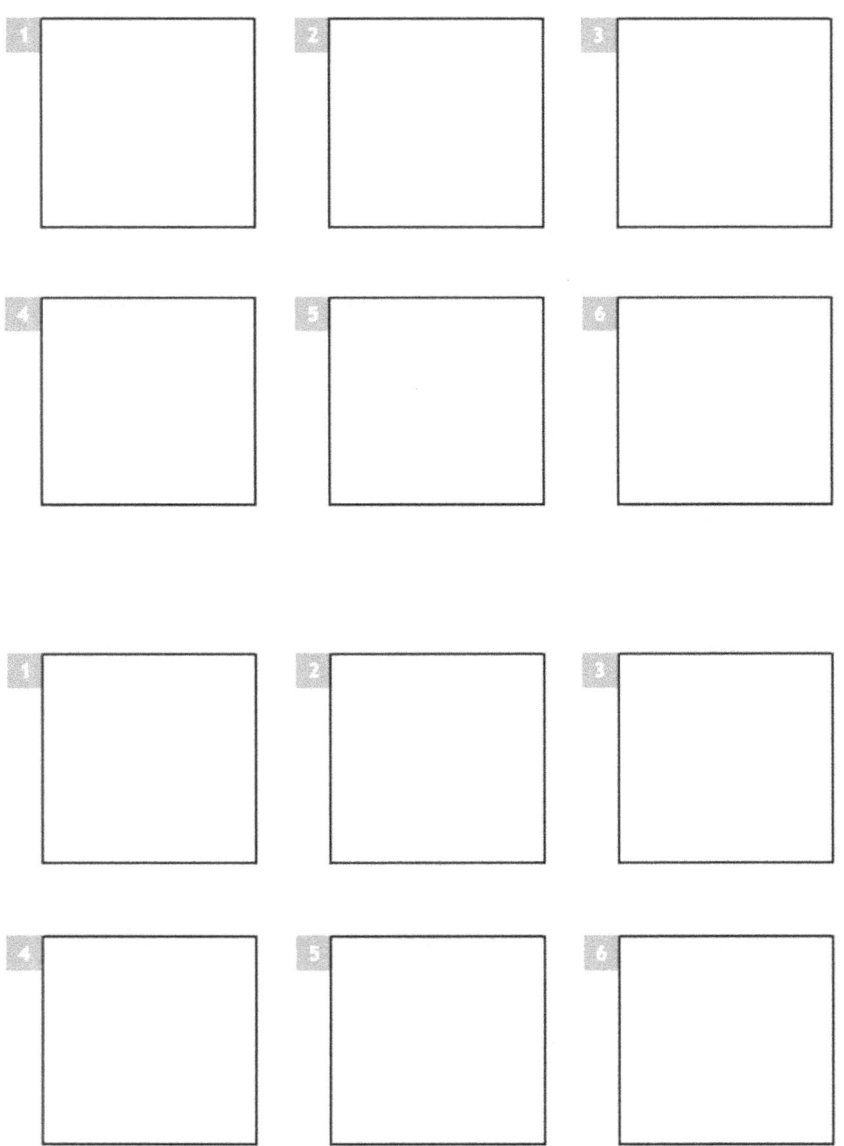

Make Your Own Doodle
Using the Pattern

Pattern #31: Orlique

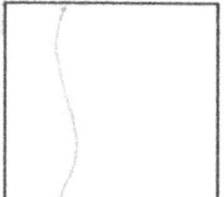 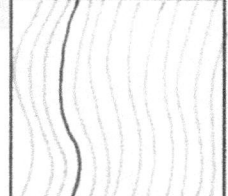 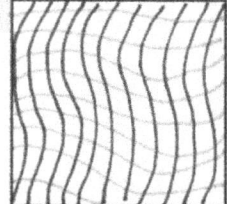

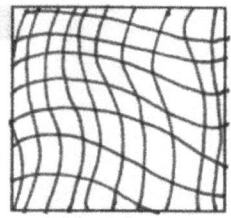

Practice the Steps Below

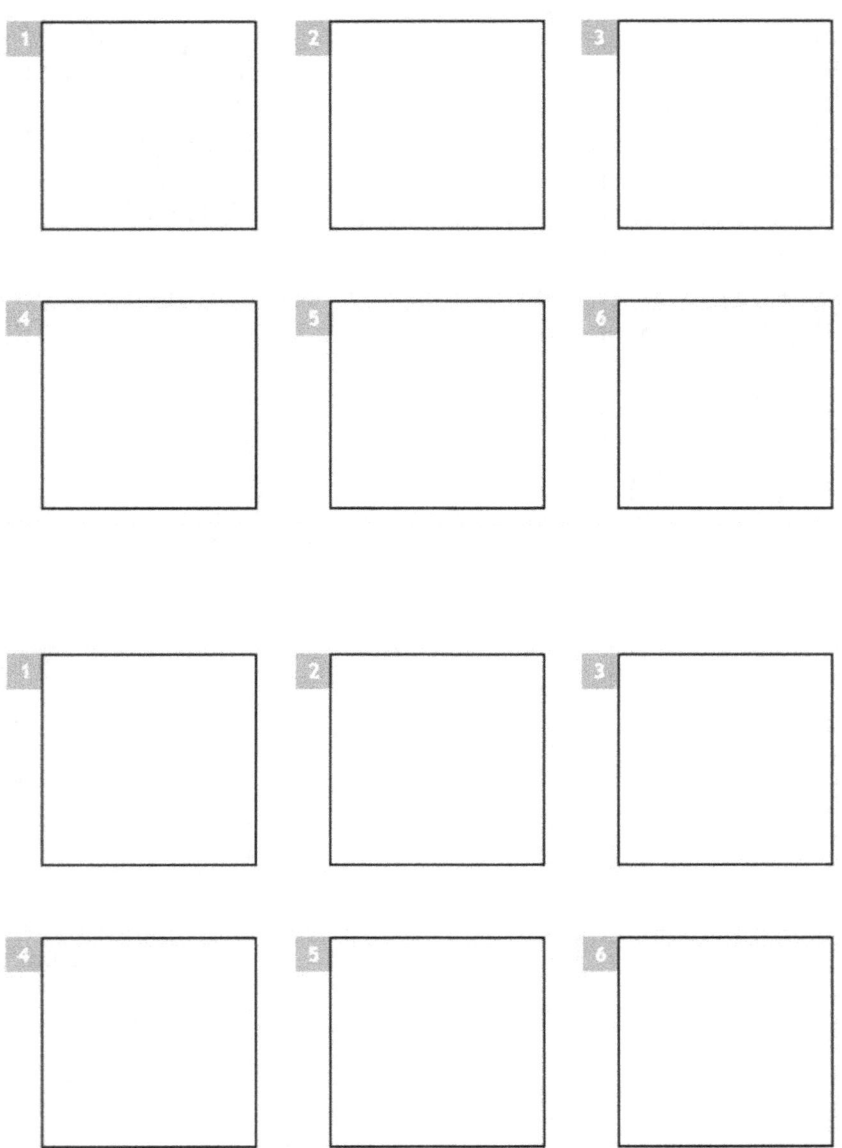

Make Your Own Doodle

Using the Pattern

Pattern #32: Wadical

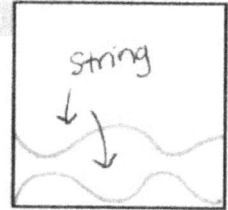 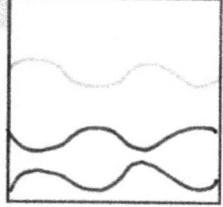 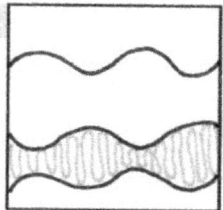

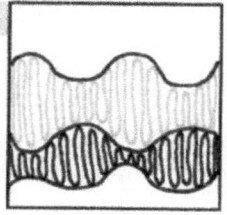 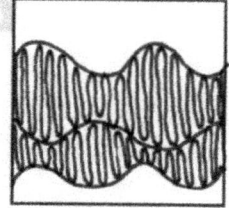

Practice the Steps Below

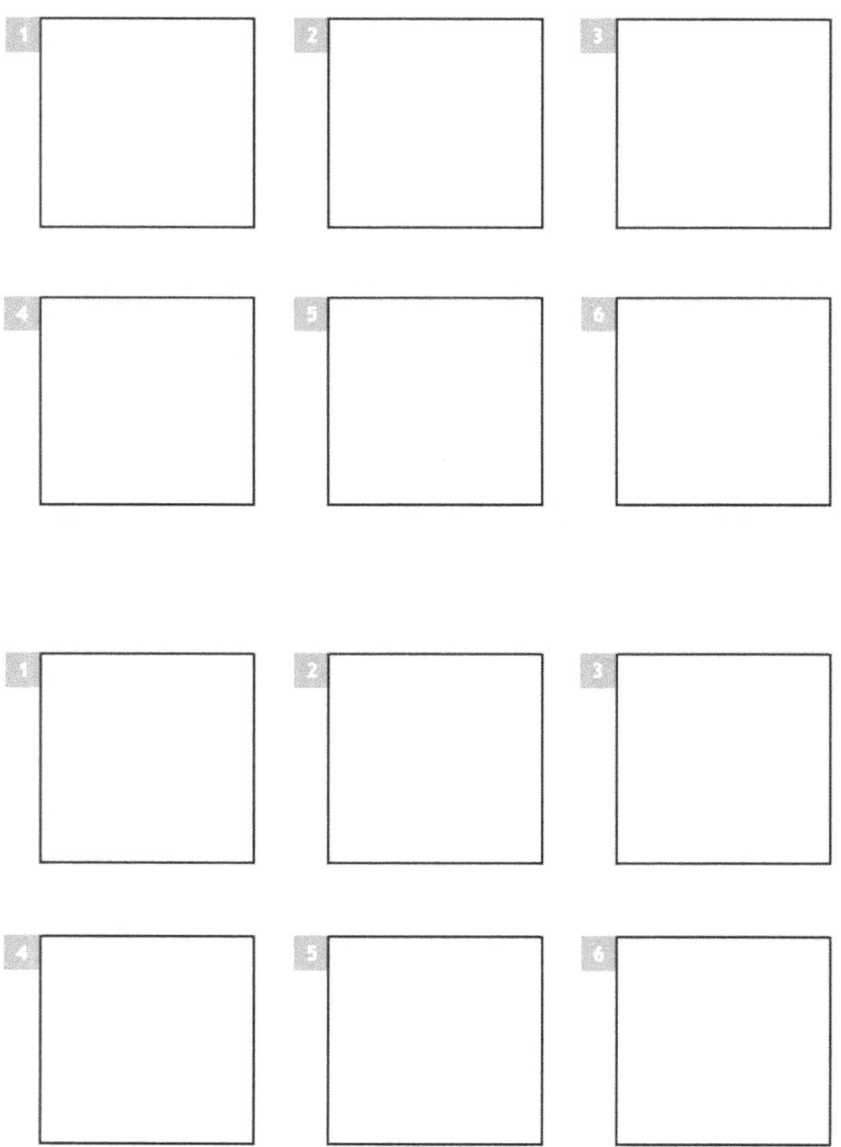

Make Your Own Doodle
Using the Pattern

Pattern #33: Festune

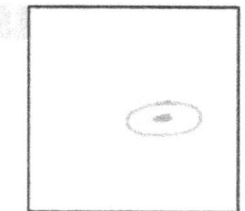 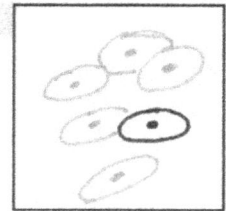 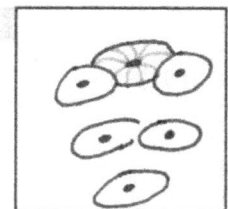

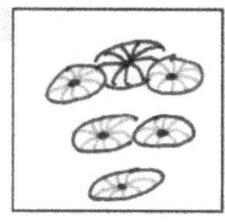 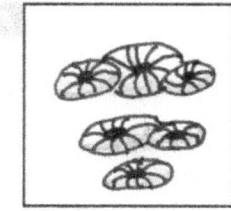

Practice the Steps Below

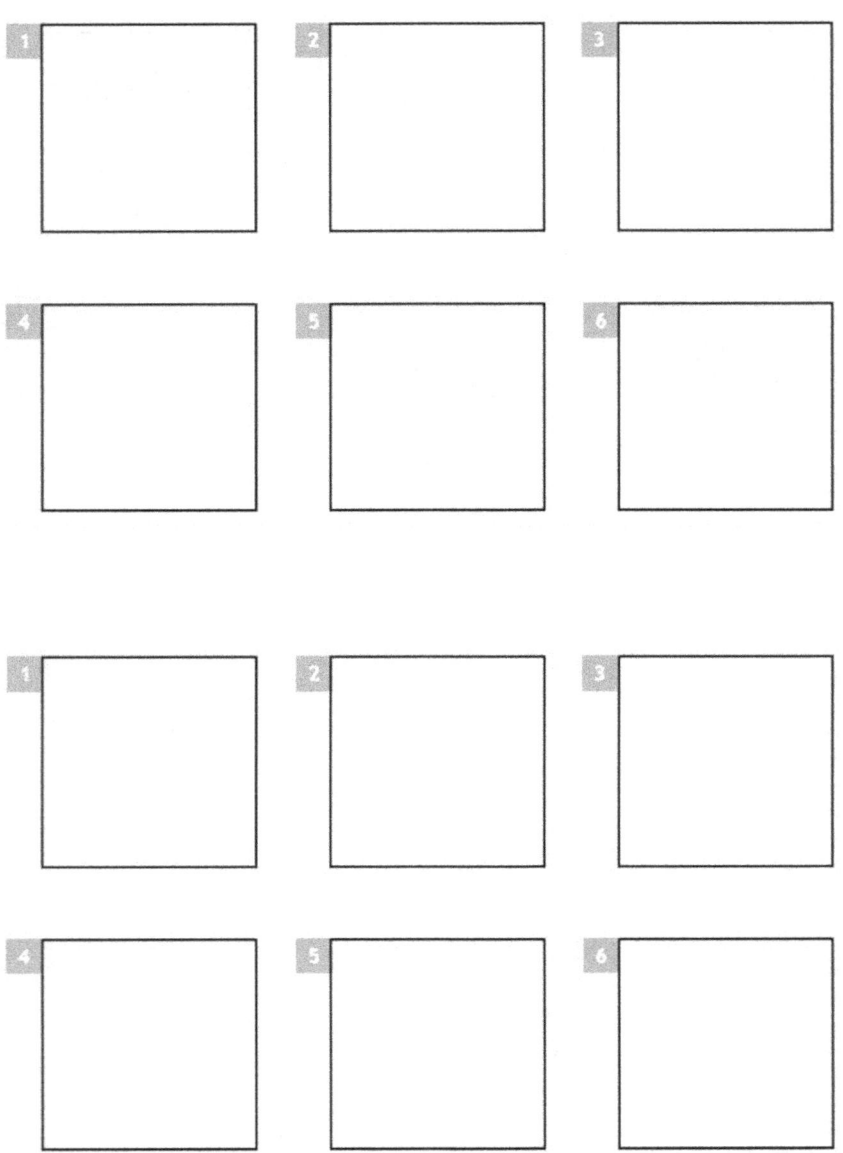

Make Your Own Doodle

Using the Pattern

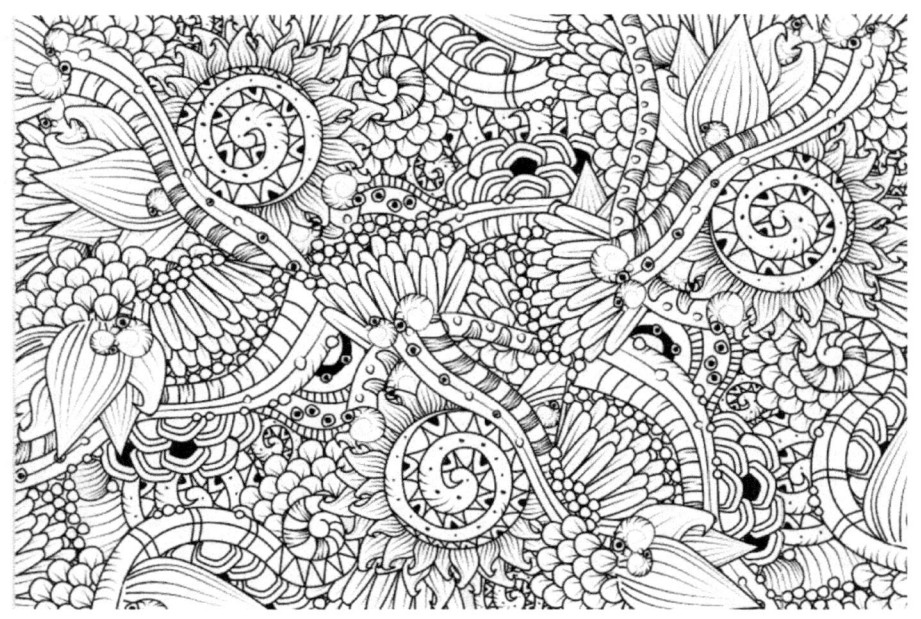

Putting It All Together

Now that you're familiar with the Zendoodle Method and all of its ins and outs...all it takes is practice. These patterns might be a little intimidating or hard at first, but I promise once you get the hang of it, it'll be easy.

It's fine for now if you have to look at the step by step pictures to figure the doodles out—that's exactly why they're here for you. But don't use them as a crutch and rule book for all things Zendoodle. The most important lesson in all of this is *get creative and be yourself.*

Once you're familiar with the style of each doodle...start to play around and make it your own. You'll be amazed at what you can create by thinking outside the lines, so to speak.

Zendoodle From the Heart

Remember, one of the foremost "rules" in Zendoodle, is that there are NO mistakes! Take this belief and embrace it. Let it put your mind at ease and free you from the constraints of fitting your art into a box.

Zendoodle artwork isn't meant to be cookie cutter. Sure, a lot of the base patterns are the same from drawing to drawing...but it never *looks* like it, does it? That's because every single person puts their own unique spin on a pattern, whether they're trying to or not.

I think that's one of the most beautiful aspects of Zendoodle: the freedom to just be **you.** In the moment. Carefree and creative. Isn't that one of the best feelings?

So although there are "rules" and methods and techniques throughout this book...they're just guidelines. Nothing is set in stone.

From here, practice your patterns and get comfortable with the strokes—draw each line confidently across your paper. There are **no** mistakes and **no** excuses!

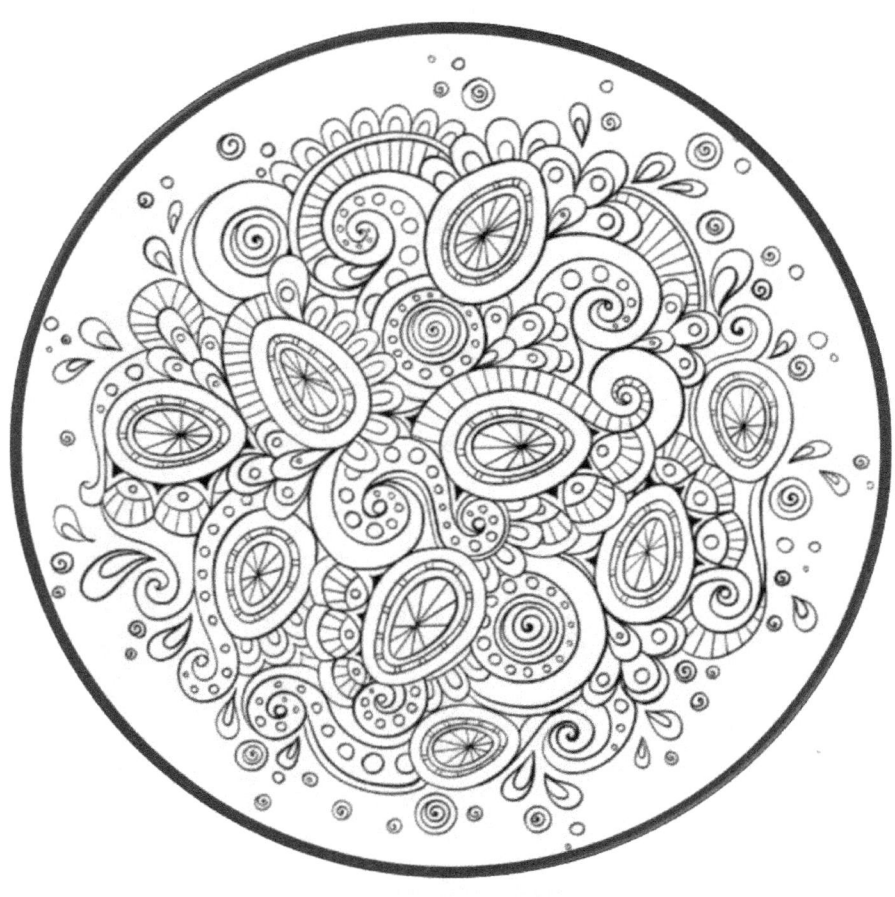

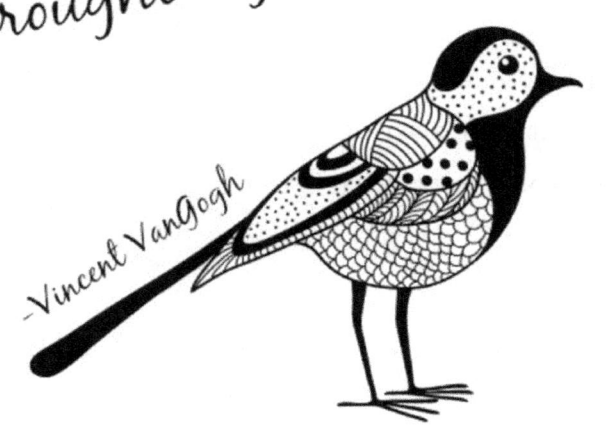

"Great things are done,
by a series of small things
brought together."

-Vincent VanGogh

Conclusion

In our everyday lives, we're all busy. We rush from here to there, never really stopping to think about the effect all the hustle and bustle has on our minds.

We never give our brains a rest. From the time we wake up to the time we fall asleep we're consumed with thoughts and ideas and annoyances and to-do's. Even when we're asleep our brain is working hard to keep our body functioning properly.

Rarely do we take time for ourselves—but boy, do we need to! If there has ever been in a time in history when our minds need a break...it's now! We are bombarded with knowledge and ideas every minute of every day. If we meditate, that's a plus...at least we're getting that time to recharge and unplug. The problem, though, is that many of us don't practice regular meditation.

That's why I'm such an advocate for Zendoodle! It's the perfect way to practice being mindful and in a way, meditate, without actually feeling like we're just "wasting" time.

It might feel like you're simply creating beautiful pictures, but the benefits extend far beyond the beauty that we can see on our pages.

I encourage you, if you haven't done so already, to take a few minutes to practice your doodles. Try to do it daily. Even if it's just 5 or 10 minutes. I have a feeling if you give it the chance it deserves, you'll find yourself addicted to the process and won't want to stop.

I hope that this book has inspired you to take on the art of Zendoodle and to create your own idea of something beautiful to share with the world.

Happy doodling,
Olivia

P.S. If you're interested in learning more about me or would like to check out my other books, then please visit my Amazon Author Central page.

www.ingramcontent.com/pod-product-compliance
Lightning Source LLC
Chambersburg PA
CBHW051918170526
45168CB00001B/446